Collaboration in Libraries and Learning Environments

Also from Facet Publishing

Maxine Melling and Joyce Little, editors
Building a Successful Customer-Service Culture: A guide for library and information managers
Facet Publishing; 2002; 978-1-85604-449-3

Margaret Weaver, editor
Transformative Learning Support Models in Higher Education
Facet Publishing; 2008; 978-1-85604-644-2

Collaboration in Libraries and Learning Environments

Edited by

Maxine Melling and Margaret Weaver

f facet publishing

Published by Facet Publishing,
7 Ridgmount Street, London WC1E 7AE
www.facetpublishing.co.uk

Facet Publishing is wholly owned by CILIP: the Chartered Institute of Library and
Information Professionals.

British Library Cataloguing in Publication Data
A catalogue record for this book is available from the British Library.

ISBN 978-1-85604-858-3

First published 2013

Text printed on FSC accredited material.

Mixed Sources
Product group from well-managed
forests and other controlled sources
www.fsc.org Cert no. SA-COC-1565
© 1996 Forest Stewardship Council

Typeset from editors' files by Flagholme Publishing Services in 10/13pt University
Old Style and Chantilly
Printed and made in Great Britain by MPG Books Group, UK.

Contents

Contributors

Rebecca Davies is Pro-Vice-Chancellor for Student and Staff Services at Aberystwyth University. Rebecca is a graduate of Aberystwyth University where she studied Librarianship and Education and also completed a Postgraduate Certificate in Education. Almost 20 years later she returned to Aberystwyth as Director of Information Services and was appointed Pro-Vice-Chancellor in 2011. Prior to this appointment she was the Head of the Assembly Library and Public Enquiry Service for the Welsh Government. Her early career focused on health information provision and research, and included: working within a health promotion unit, as Nursing Librarian at Trinity College, Carmarthen, as researcher at the Department of Information Studies, Aberystwyth University, and as Health Science Librarian for the School of Health Science, University of Wales, Swansea. Rebecca is passionate about libraries, using technology to make life easier and delivering excellent services.

Rachel Esson is Associate Director, Library Academic Services, at Victoria University of Wellington Library (New Zealand). Prior to this role, Rachel was Head of Research and Learning Services at Victoria and worked in a number of roles at the library of Otago University Medical School. She has an MLIS in Library and Information Studies and a Postgraduate Certificate in Tertiary Teaching. Rachel has written and published in the field of evaluation and impact, and is passionate about leadership development and student-centred library service delivery.

Craig Gaskell is Principal of the University of Hull's Scarborough Campus. He obtained a first-class honours degree in Computer Science in 1991, a Higher Education Teaching Diploma in 1996 and a PhD (via part-time study) in 1997, all from the University of Hull. Between 1994 and 1999 he held Lectureships, first in Computer Science at the University of Hull, and then in Software Engineering at Durham. In 1999 he moved to University College Scarborough (UCS) to take up a Principal Lectureship and the post of founding head of the University of Hull Centre for Internet Computing. UCS merged with the University of Hull in 2000, and he continued as Head of Centre for a further five years. In 2005 he was appointed Dean of the University of Hull's Scarborough Campus and he became Campus Principal in October 2010. Craig is a Chartered Engineer and remains actively involved in the accreditation of Computer Science degree programmes nationally via the British Computer Society. His most recent research activity has focused on leadership, management and change in higher education (HE), with a specific focus on developing a better understanding of the strategies and structures of satellite HE campuses.

Raegan Hiles is the Policy and Public Affairs Manager at AMOSSHE, The Student Services Organisation. She has held posts across the UK HE sector including at a higher education institution (HEI), and at the Higher Education Funding Council for England (HEFCE), where she was the policy officer in the central Research Assessment Exercise (RAE) management team, a policy advisor to several RAE panels, and worked on library and researcher issues as a policy advisor in the Research Policy Team. Raegan is well versed in the professional organization sector in HE, being the national lead at AMOSSHE, working closely with the Association of University Administrators (AUA) and having formerly been on the Association of Research Managers and Administrators (ARMA) training subcommittee. She has also worked with representatives of SCONUL (the Society of College, National and University Libraries) on researcher mobility issues while in the HEFCE Research Policy team, and designed and delivered professional project management training materials for HEFCE. She is currently conducting research into the role, reach, purpose and benefits of professional HE organizations in the UK and Canada.

Liz Jolly is Director of Library and Information Services at Teesside University. Previously she was Associate Director (Services and Operations) in Information and Learning Services at the University of Salford. She has held departmental senior management positions at East London and London South Bank universities and has also worked at Huddersfield, Leeds Metropolitan, Lincoln and Manchester Metropolitan universities. Liz is a Fellow both of the Chartered Institute of Library and Information Professionals (CILIP) and the Royal Society for the encouragement of Arts, Manufactures and Commerce (RSA). She has been a Trustee of CILIP and has chaired the CILIP University, College and Research Group. Liz is currently Vice-Chair of SCONUL, a member of the Editorial Board of the *New Review of Academic Librarianship* and a member of the British Library Advisory Council.

Dr Ruth Kifer has served since 2005 as Dean of the University Library at San José State University in California. In collaboration with the San José Public Library, the university opened an innovative university–city library in 2003. As university library dean, She collaborates with the director of the San José Public Library system to define a shared vision, and to offer effective, quality library services and information resources to both the university and the broader San José community. Ruth previously served as associate university librarian for distributed libraries at George Mason University in Fairfax, Virginia, where she was responsible for the administration of three of the university's libraries, including the Johnson Center Library, another innovative library that tested She limits of 'library-as-place' as early as 1996. Ruth has a master's degree in Library Science from the University of Pittsburgh in Pennsylvania and a Juris Doctorate degree from the University of Baltimore in Maryland.

Maxine Melling is Pro-Vice Chancellor (Operations) at the University of Gloucestershire (UK). She was until recently Director of Library and Student Support at Liverpool John Moores University, where she was responsible for the leadership of student administration services, student finance, library and archives and computing support. Her professional background is in library and information services in further and higher education. She has published in the fields of quality management, staff development and training, customer services and support for e-learning. Her current interests lie in collaborative working to support the student experience and she is researching the different ways in which universities work across traditional boundaries. Maxine has been proactive in the development of cross-institutional and cross-sectoral collaboration and shared services. She has chaired the North West Academic Libraries Group, has represented higher education libraries on Libraries North West and was the inaugural chair of the Northern Collaboration group. She is a Trustee of the Gladstone Library in Hawarden and is a consultant for the Leadership Foundation for Higher Education (LFHE), supporting institutions in leadership of the student experience.

Dave Pattern is the Library Systems Manager at the University of Huddersfield, with responsibility for the continuing development of the web services and facilities provided by the library. A web developer with over 15 years of experience, he previously worked for a major UK library book supplier before joining Huddersfield as the lead developer on the JISC-funded INHALE and INFORMS projects. Since 2004, he has been responsible for incorporating a variety of 2.0 enhancements into the OPAC and developing in-house services, as well as setting up weblogs and wikis for the library. He is a committed '2.0' advocate and was named as one of the '2009 Movers and Shakers' by the *Library Journal* and is the

2011 *Information World Review* 'Information Professional of the Year'. Dave represents the University on the Serials Solutions Advisory Board and is Chair of the UK Serials Solutions User Group.

Michael Ridley was, until January 2012, the Chief Information Officer and Chief Librarian at the University of Guelph (Ontario, Canada). He has worked as a librarian since 1979, holding positions at the University of Guelph, McMaster University and the University of Waterloo. He has served as the President of the Canadian Association for Information Science, President of the Ontario Library Association and Chair of the Ontario Council of University Libraries. Michael has been a member of the Board of the Canadian Association of Research Libraries (CARL), the Canadian Research Knowledge Network (CRKN) and the Canadian University Council of CIOs (CUCCIO). Currently he is serving on the Board of Directors of the Ontario Research and Innovation Optical Network (ORION) and the Board of Governors of the University of Guelph. In 2010 he was awarded the Miles Blackwell Award for Outstanding Academic Librarian by the Canadian Library Association.

Sue Roberts is CEO and State Librarian of the State Library of Victoria in Melbourne, Australia. Prior to moving to Melbourne, she was University Librarian at Victoria University of Wellington in New Zealand and Dean of Learning Services at Edge Hill University in the UK. Sue was born in Leigh, Lancashire (UK), and studied English at the University of Leicester before postgraduate studies in library and information management. She has worked in a variety of library and learning services roles within the higher education sector. Sue has also researched and published in the fields of library management and leadership and is the co-author of *Managing Information Services: the changing role of the academic librarian* (Facet Publishing, 2004), *Developing the New Learning Environment: the changing role of the academic librarian* (Facet Publishing, 2005) and *Leadership: the challenge for the information profession* (Facet Publishing, 2008).

Graham Stone is Information Resources Manager at the University of Huddersfield and has 18 years' experience of working in academic libraries. He is responsible for the library information resources budget, the management and operation of the Acquisitions and Journals and Electronic Resources teams and the University Repository. He is also leading the University of Huddersfield Press initiative. Graham has managed a number of Joint Information Systems Committee (JISC) projects including the Library Impact Data Project (LIDP), Huddersfield Open Access Publishing (HOAP) and Huddersfield, Intota, KnowledgeBase+ Evaluation (HIKE). He is Publications Officer of the UK Serials Group (UKSG), a member of the *Insights* editorial board, the Electronic Information Resources Working Group (EIRWG), the Publisher and Library Solutions Working Group (PALS) metadata and interoperability working group, and chair of the JISC Journal Archives Advisory Board. Graham is currently undertaking research for a Doctor of Enterprise (EntD).

Margaret Weaver is Head of Library and Student Services at the University of Cumbria. She is a chartered member of the CILIP and a Fellow of the Higher Education Academy. She has worked at a number of north-west universities, and while at Huddersfield University led the groundbreaking JISC project on the creation of a national interactive web-based information skills service. Margaret has written and presented widely on the pedagogy of learning spaces, integrated learning support and super-converged services. She is the editor of a recent book on this subject: *Transformative Learning Support Models in Higher Education: educating the whole student* (Facet Publishing, 2008). In 2011 she led the Higher Education Academy Change Academy COLLABORATE! project examining shared academic library services, centred on collaboration between partners in universities in the north of England. She is currently Chair of the North West Academic Libraries (NoWAL) group.

Dr Andrew West is Director of Student Services at the University of Sheffield. His remit has a wide scope covering the student lifecycle - including student recruitment, admissions, registry, student administration, learning and teaching strategy and support, and a broad range of student support services. Andrew served as Vice-Chair of AMOSSHE, The Student Services Organisation from 2010 to 2012, and was Vice-Chair of AUA from 2010 to 2011. He also serves as a member of the HE Advisory Panel for the Office of the Independent Adjudicator. His work on student affairs and management and leadership issues has been published in professional journals and other publications, including a chapter on strategy and service quality within UNESCO's guide to global best practice in student services, and a recent piece on staff development in a practitioners' guide to improving the student experience.

Introduction

Those responsible for delivering library and support services are dealing with unprecedented change as countries, sectors and individuals face challenge and uncertainty brought about by major shifts in financial and fiscal policies. Higher education and other public institutions are responding strategically and with vigour to this challenge and universities and colleges are developing new ways of working with others, to provide better value for money and to maintain and enhance the student experience. In parallel, ubiquitous web technologies are enabling fundamental shifts in relationships between students, staff and institutions, creating a learning experience that is more student-led and founded on communities of online collaborators.

This book of essays recognizes and uncovers the innovations that leaders and practitioners are implementing to transform and develop the provision of sustainable and creative support services. Such innovations are resulting in diverse models of delivery, including the convergence of many different student-facing services, innovative approaches to the use of IT and the development of more active collaborative networks and commercial partnerships. This collection of accounts from the UK, USA, Canada and Australasia considers the changing context and the broad principles affecting the ways in which we need to manage and provide services, and also offers alternative methods, written by experts in their field.

Because this book advocates and addresses the need to work across traditional boundaries, the authors include professionals from outside library and information services as well as those responsible for leading multiply converged or joint service teams. The editors believe that it is only by getting into a real conversation with such colleagues and by looking at alternative approaches to providing support, especially during times of adversity, that we can be successful in meeting the changing needs and expectations of users of our services in a cost-effective manner.

The authors of the chapters in this volume are working within a rapidly changing environment, influenced by the global economy, government intervention and increasing client expectations. The premise of this book is that the options available might be either to become insular, emphasizing specialist skills and communities, or (as we advocate) to broaden one's mission and vision, recognizing that collaboration can enrich services by introducing new ways of doing things, creating possibilities through economies of scale and through purposefully subjecting plans, thoughts and processes to partnership working. Most importantly, collaboration can serve as a way of representing services from the user's viewpoint and not from that of the service provider.

Chapter 1 of the volume is written in a personal, engaging style, by Rebecca Davies, one of the senior figures in UK higher education. This persuasive, thought-provoking chapter sets the scene for the entire book, with complex themes developed from examples inside and outside the university sector. These themes demonstrate the openness of our world, the fluid 'edgeless environment', the seismic boundary shift caused by developments in social media, e-publishing and technology, leading to completely new relationships with our customers (students and staff), that ultimately affect all our lives inside and outside work. The author challenges the usual idea of what a modern library (or even a university) is for, leading on to her recommendations on where the profession should focus its efforts to become future proof. She argues that in order for success, library and information services units need to maximize the opportunities for collaboration at every level (individually, professionally, educationally) as a risk mitigation strategy against uncertainty and also to ensure relevance to the goals of our institutions. There are many stories and pictures in the chapter that connect to the chapters that follow. After reading Chapter 1 we think you will want to read more and be in no doubt that our collective future is a bright one.

In Chapter 2, Craig Gaskell discusses a radical restructuring which aimed to shift the focus of the Campus away from internal structures and towards a student perspective. The author discusses the increasingly important part played by the so-called student voice in the delivery of higher education and how new ways of configuring and delivering services can add value to the student experience, ensuring that students work in partnership in developing their services

Chapter 2 also considers the challenges associated with a growing consumer culture and student expectations. Issues addressed include changing student perceptions and how the national debate on fees in the UK has affected local practice and how service delivery has responded.

In Chapter 3 Andrew West and Raegan Hiles discuss the role of professional associations in providing guidance and support to higher education leaders. The authors provide an overview of the complex environment of professional associations and consider their relevance in supporting leaders working across traditional structural boundaries. In addition they discuss how the associations themselves are starting to work across boundaries through mergers, shared governance models or joint projects.

In Chapter 4 Michael Ridley considers the cultures and values that underpin collaborative working, using three major collaborative ventures in Canada to provide practical examples of the issues under discussion. The author argues that collaboration is often driven by adversity and, to be successful, needs to offer mutual self-interest to those involved. The author emphasizes that the true values and culture of an organization are revealed in the actions of its staff and in its policies and procedures. When working collaboratively there is a challenge to negotiate different value systems and to articulate clearly how the consortia will operate and how this will impact on staff. Michael Ridley argues for a very open consideration of values when agreeing to form collaborative groups. Some of the prerequisites to success that he considers are the need for trust and mutual understanding, an acknowledgement of differential benefits, an acceptance of some loss of control and agreed shared objectives. This is a pragmatic chapter, grounded in real experience of developing successful joint ventures. The author emphasizes that all parties involved in collaborative ventures should be open about fears or conflict and should be realistic about what can be achieved.

In Chapter 5 Margaret Weaver describes how one group of senior library leaders in the north of England attempted to achieve complex change, creating the vision and impetus for a new strategic grouping of academic libraries. The group sought to harness the creative thinking and change-management approaches offered by the Change Academy process. The author analyses the process and outcomes that enabled the new Northern Collaboration of HE libraries to be sustained and to see a shared future, during a time of unprecedented change in higher education in the UK.

Reflecting on the opportunities for new ways of communicating, thinking and working, the author (as the Change Academy COLLABORATE! leader) offers unique insights into the political and leadership aspects of introducing and managing change across diverse mission groups. The skills and techniques required are of relevance to other change leaders seeking to unlock the creative potential in uncertain situations and in the volatile environment in which library and information services (and universities) find themselves. It is argued that during times of uncertainty more ways of thinking about change are needed, in destabilizing situations, to reveal viable options and models. The author establishes a new idea for libraries, that of the collaboration paradox, which, like the agitation felt by the pearl in the oyster, leads to constructive forms of structure, service and relationships underpinned by collaboration.

In Chapter 6 Sue Roberts and Rachel Esson explore the significance of leadership in a climate of increasing global uncertainty and assess how practitioners in library and information environments can equip themselves to maximize their impact and influence. They argue that being able to lead collaboratively is likely to be the single biggest enabler in their achieving future success. Several models from the leadership literature are used to illustrate those qualities that are needed (and that should be nurtured) to cope with the many new demands of an increasingly online and complex world. Their insights into the 'inner game' of leadership make a compelling case for individuals in leadership roles at all levels of the organization to become critically self-aware, flexible, open to cultural diversity and to be able to recognize potential in themselves and in others. Leading the unfamiliar, adapting to power shifts, examining core values and spinning a creative web of interpersonal connections are more likely to be successful in collaborative contexts. Chapter 6 is thus one of the key integrating chapters in the book, drawing together the behaviours and mindsets that are needed to lead collaboratively across organizational boundaries in a sustainable and effective manner. In summary, the chapter is an empowering read for existing and future leaders.

Chapter 7 gives an analytical overview of a decade of library technology development, led by Huddersfield University, UK. Graham Stone and Dave Pattern, renowned experts and innovators, explore how collaboration has enabled this work to happen and how collaborative tools, which are now ubiquitous in the Web and Library 2.0 environment, are shaping students' experience of their academic library. Underpinning the many projects explained is the role that personalization, the sharing of data and games-based learning (Lemon Tree) play in engaging and understanding students and researchers. Huddersfield was the first UK institution to find a link between library data and student attainment. The authors highlight how they successfully used partnership working to triangulate their results across the world. Shared services are briefly touched on in the context of next-generation library management systems.

A fundamental point is made about the creative, liberating culture and senior management drive needed to allow time for library-staff experimentation, training and adaptation of tools to the local context. Projects are shown to benefit from strategic alliances with a range of partnerships: technology companies, the UK JISC and other academic libraries. Quotations from thought leaders in the technology arena root the chapter in the real world, demonstrating the relevance, value and impact of the library nationally and internationally through collaborative communities of practice.

Chapter 8 charts the development of 'place' in academic libraries and in particular learning-space design as an enabler and facilitator of learning. Liz Jolly outlines the changing relationships that are resulting between libraries and their institutions, libraries and students, and libraries and professional support services, drawing on notable examples of library designs and projects in the UK and USA. What is fundamental to this chapter is the emergence of library-space research as a discipline in its own right. The author calls for a more rigorous approach in understanding the learning that takes place in our modern, boundary-free spaces.

Liz also considers the collaborations needed to deliver what she terms the 'library design continuum', pointing to the need to meet the diverse study requirements of our students, ranging from quiet and traditional spaces through to collaborative, flexible, dynamic learning spaces. The literature reviewed provides a rich overview of modern library environments that have learning at the core. Key questions are posed about the future of the library, including implications for library leadership, and Liz concludes that libraries (and librarians) are in a central position to influence their institutional strategies and place the library even more firmly at the heart of student learning in higher education.

Chapter 9 looks at the background to the development of so-called super-converged services, the drivers for this change and the challenges and opportunities faced in providing them. The term 'super-convergence' is gaining recognition in describing the bringing together of a range of services, either structurally or in front-of-house delivery. In this chapter Maxine Melling acknowledges that converged service delivery is not new, but points to a change in emphasis and range of coverage which is developing across the higher education sector in the UK. In common with other authors she cites national drivers for change, but emphasizes the importance of local context and, in common with other contributors to this volume of essays, highlights that the approaches to collaboration should be based very closely on local needs and culture.

The author argues strongly for service delivery that is based on the viewpoint of the user or customer, removing the need for users to navigate structures that have been put in place for the convenience of the organization. In considering the development of super-converged services, Maxine highlights a number of issues that link to themes across the book, including the development of 'advanced generalist staff', the role of the professional associations in supporting non-traditional organizations and the need for a different approach to leadership in a so-called cold climate.

In Chapter 10 Ruth Kifer discusses the phenomenon of joint-use libraries over the past decade in the USA and elsewhere worldwide. Joint-use libraries are created between public libraries and university libraries, between public schools and public libraries, between community colleges and universities, and between any library organizations wishing to collaborate on the delivery of library services. These collaborations exist as a result of institutions of higher education and other entities making the bold decision to work across organizational boundaries for the benefit of their respective library communities and to make best use of limited revenues. The joint organizations that are created embrace a broader view of mission and vision than do organizations with a more traditional and sometimes insular view of their reason for being. The chapter chronicles joint-use libraries with different models of administration and funding, of varying sizes and in different geographic locations.

Chapter 10 focuses primarily on the joint university and public library created between San José State University and the San José Public Library in San José, California, the heart of Silicon Valley. Now in its eighth year of operation the Dr Martin Luther King, Jr. Library has provided stellar library services, technological innovation and access to print and digital collections for the fifth largest campus in the California State University system and the tenth largest city in the USA. The discussion outlines the planning process employed to develop the joint library and explore the staffing issues, user perceptions, budgetary matters and other factors involved in operating a joint-use library.

Although all the authors see the benefits of collaboration there is no one blueprint. Rather, the national and international contributors represent a state of mind or openness to different ways of working which cross traditional professional, structural and institutional boundaries. Even so, it is striking that, although authors represent different countries, professions and roles, common themes emerge in relation to the drivers for change, the culture and values necessary to work collaboratively, the leadership and staff skills needed and a clear commitment to placing the student or client at the centre of service delivery.

Maxine Melling, Pro-Vice Chancellor (Operations),
University of Gloucestershire
Margaret Weaver, Head of Library and Student Services,
University of Cumbria

Abbreviations

ACPA	College Student Educators International
ACRL	Association of College and Research Libraries
ADSHE	Association of Dyslexia Specialists in Higher Education
AHUA	Association of Heads of University Administrators
AISA	Association of International Student Advisors
ARC	Academic Registrars Council
AUA	Association of University Administrators
AUCC	Association for University and College Counselling
AUDE	Association of University Directors of Estates
AUPO	Association of University Procurement Officers
BAHSHE	British Association of Healthcare Services for Students in Higher Education
BUFDG	British Universities Finance Directors Group
BUILA	British Universities' International Liaison Association
CA	Change Academy
CALIM	Consortium of Academic Libraries in Manchester
CETL	Centre for Excellence in Teaching and Learning
CILASS	Centre for Inquiry-Based Learning in the Arts and Social Sciences
CILIP	Chartered Institute of Library and Information Professionals
CNSLP	Canadian National Site Licensing Project
CopacAD	Copac Activity Data Project
COU	Council of Ontario Universities
CPD	continuing professional development
CRKN	Canadian Research Knowledge Network
ECU	Equality Challenge Unit
HEA	Higher Education Academy

HEFCE	Higher Education Funding Council for England
HEI	higher education institution
HELOA	Higher Education Liaison Officers Association
HEPI	Higher Education Policy Institute
HUCS	Heads of University Counselling Services
IASAS	International Association of Student Affairs Services
JISC	Joint Information Systems Committee
KIS	Key Information Sets
LFHE	Leadership Foundation for Higher Education
LIBER	Ligue des Bibliothèques Européennes de Recherche – Association of European Research Libraries
LIDP	Library Impact Data Project
NADP	National Association of Disability Practitioners
NASMA	National Association of Student Money Advisors
NASPA	Student Affairs Administrators in Higher Education
NC	Northern Collaboration
NEYAL	North-East and Yorkshire Academic Libraries
NoWAL	North-West Academic Libraries
NSS	National Students Survey
NUS	National Union of Students
OCUL	Ontario Council of University Libraries
PARN	Professional Associations Research Network
QAA	Quality Assurance Agency
QSN	Quality Strategy Network
RCUK	Research Councils UK
REF	Research Excellence Framework
RIN	Research Information Network
SCONUL	Society of College, National and University Libraries
SEDA	Staff and Educational Development Association
TUG	TriUniversity Group of Libraries
UCAS	Universities and Colleges Admissions Service
UCISA	Universities and Colleges Information Systems Association
UKCISA	UK Council for International Student Affairs
UUK	Universities UK

1 The changing higher education context

Rebecca Davies, Aberystwyth University, UK

Introduction

This chapter will focus on how we prepare for the changing environment(s) for higher education institutions (HEIs), with particular note to libraries and professional support services. I have attempted to scan the current horizon, as all wise clairvoyants do, and consider what it means to be a student or staff member in an HEI so that I can map possible options for future success and highlight implications for collaboration and new ways of working.

Why are we here?

It is always tempting to create a complex picture of where we are and why we exist by focusing on intricate definitions of our current landscape. However, setting off on a brave march by looking at our feet is a sure way to stumble and fall. As a keen walker with particularly poor balance I have learned, to my cost, not to focus on each footfall or to over-think how to avoid each small rock I need to transverse. Instead, by focusing on the distant path ahead, I can avoid painful mistakes and prepare for the big challenges or cliffs. Therefore, rather than spending significant time analysing 'why we are here' this chapter focuses on the path ahead.

My simple view of our starting point is that the purpose of higher education is to service, enable and deliver teaching, learning and research.

Information professionals and universities have an exceptional capacity to exploit uncertainties to thrive. In the same ways as professionals in agriculture and manufacturing changed what was possible during their respective revolutions, university library and information services staff have developed services and tools that exploit the advancing information age.

By playing our part in this revolution, we've seen creativity, communication, ingenuity and collaboration in ways that we couldn't have dreamed of. More people now browse university library journals from their homes and offices than ever used the paper copies. Timetables are accessed via the web and travel times to meetings are cut down to a stroll to a video-conferencing suite on campus or a Skype™ call in the park on a mobile device. We simply can't imagine a time when we were restricted by paper needing to be transported from one place to another – try to think back to times when memos hadn't yet become e-mails and written feedback from conferences was delivered months after the event, as opposed to real-time Twitter feeds.

So how does it feel?

When attempting to develop models for the future I recognize that we work within a context where we can be certain of our uncertainties – so, in the future universities will service, enable and deliver teaching, learning and research for students and academics who they don't yet know (so can't understand), who will want to use technologies that have not yet been developed, and will be working under policies and governments not yet formed. Working with uncertainty is our new 'normal state', so for each of the areas considered in this chapter which form part of our working environment I have identified key opportunities where collaboration can help future success.

Decisions we make today have an impact decades from now; the library buildings cherished (or despised) on our campus may have been built before we were born, yet influence the National Student Survey (NSS) scores we receive in 2012. The decision today to cease a particular discipline or to introduce a new one will affect the choices available to a child born tomorrow when choosing to apply, or not, to our institution.

It takes a particular approach to be content living within such an uncertain state, where decisions have such long-term impacts. David Watson, in his book *The Question of Morale: managing happiness and unhappiness in university life*, cites a strategic discussion he had with senior academic leaders of one of the world's 'top universities' and provides the following edited statements:

- We don't have enough money to do our jobs properly, but we are really good at them.
- We are severely oppressed, but we are also happy in our work.
- The government should support higher education better, and it should do this by giving us (our university) more than them (than that other university).
- We can't give students what they really need, but it is our duty to attract the very

best to come to study with us.

- In attracting these highly qualified students, what counts is the quality of our research, not of our teaching.
- The league tables are terrible, but we must climb them, and the higher we climb the less publically we shall criticize them.

(Watson, 2009, 3)

Reflecting on these statements with some international colleagues, we all agreed that we both recognized and empathized with these statements; it appears that in my experience this is a global 'state of mind' of academic leaders.

In simple terms, as members of staff in an HEI in the 21st century we work with contradictions and make decisions which can have impacts beyond our lifetime.

Predicting the future, based on the present

Don't worry about what anybody else is going to do. The best way to predict the future is to invent it.

(Alan Kay, father of the software commercialized into the Apple Macintosh, 1971, cited by Herzfeld, 2005, 2)

I am not overconfident in my skills as a clairvoyant, but was comforted when reflecting on the work I undertook in 2000 when I was working in Library and Information Services at Swansea University. I was an advocate of (what was then) 'computer-based learning' (CBL) and I took an active role in collaborating with Dr Mike Tait (Head of Health Informatics and E-learning) and his team to exploit and understand the use of emerging technologies for learning. We conducted a review of CBL in nurse education (Lewis et al., 2001) and concluded that the most probable future use of CBL is that it:

. . . has great potential as an aid in future nursing education, with regard to:

- meeting students' educational requirements more effectively
- achieving these requirements more efficiently
- providing students who have differing learning styles with alternative representations of knowledge and with methods of assimilating that knowledge
- providing nurses with the opportunity to develop skills and confidence in the use of CBL and computers in general
- nurturing a desire to use such resources in their future careers.

Future chapters of this book explore in great depth the changing context for technology and learning – but from this simple list constructed at the turn of the last century it is interesting to reflect on the external factors, which could not have been predicted in 2000, that have affected the realization of the great potential of CBL.

The biggest 'miss' from the list is that aspirations (and hopes) for the reductions in cost (even in 2000 we used the code name 'efficiency'!) have not materialized. For example, education has not reduced in price and staff teaching-loads have not been cut. I also suspect that the desire to use eBay™ and Facebook has done more to develop 'confidence in the use of . . . computers in general' (Lewis et al., 2002, 36) than CBL ever did.

If we were using this small study to plan for libraries, teaching rooms and learning spaces, would we have got anything wrong? The list suggests we'd be saving money by using CBL, but that we would have students who demanded increased access to technology. The predicted technology requirements would have been around PC workstation rooms and network points. Who'd have figured out that the actual global demand we'd have been facing in 12 years' time was for mobile connectivity (both 3G and, increasingly, Wi-Fi only) and power sockets. If only we'd known that installing an extra couple of dozen power sockets year on year would have been a huge hit in our comments and feedback forms!

So, following that cautionary tale on my clairvoyant skills, I have sought to add some definition and colour to the future landscapes we will inhabit by considering:

- Development and decline? The globalized economic and political environment
- From local to global: changes in knowledge access and exchange
- From student experience to student expectation
- Never mind the quality, look at our rank: the influence of the league table.

Within each of these areas consideration is given to the changing and challenging context for the future of higher education. No single service or isolated individual will have the capacity to come up with solutions in our complex environment. Working alone is a risky strategy as complex issues which change rapidly require elegant, thought-through solutions which no one has the capacity to deliver alone.

Development and decline? The globalized economic and political environment

Universities operate under their institution's, their nation's and the global, political and economic arenas. Politics and economics influence our ability to service, enable and deliver teaching, learning and research. The dependence on public funding, with responsibilities to the sometimes tacit and sometimes explicit policy agendas, mean that universities react to (and with varying levels of success influence) their nation's ambitions.

Within the UK the process of devolution (with devolved governments in Northern Ireland, Scotland and Wales) has brought different policy agendas into focus. Tony Bruce noted:

> The devolution process has given the devolved countries the powers to make their own policy choices with the overall aim of securing the long term future of the United Kingdom. Whether this broader objective will be achieved seems increasingly doubtful but there is no doubt that devolution has provided the four countries with the opportunity to shape their own higher education sectors in a new direction even though these choices may have been constrained by the complexities of the devolution settlement, the existence of a UK market and the dominance of England. Whether those policy choices will lead to stronger and more competitive national systems remains to be seen.
>
> (Bruce, 2012, 101)

Students from England, Northern Ireland, Scotland and Wales face differing fee regimes for undergraduate study and a climate where the devolved nation's policy agendas are influencing the structure of universities, admission policies and social participation. The Research Councils, which administer the majority of competitive public research funding, remain predominantly at a UK-wide level. For universities used to collaborating (and/or competing) with each other there are now distinct policies which need to be taken into account when working across the devolved borders.

Beyond UK borders we are now working in an increasingly international educational community, as depicted by other writers in this book. For students there could be some significant opportunities – potentially a global market can lead to increased choice and improved quality. As globalization matures, and if universities follow the experience of other sectors, we will see the domination of a few select brands and a possible 'franchise' model created by international mergers and acquisitions sitting under a small number of huge, global corporations akin to global fast-food outlets and/or shopping malls. Quality and customer experience in global corporations are carefully policed to ensure the same look and feel wherever you are; brand identity is protected, with occasional acknowledgements of local custom or culture. A university which operates as a multinational corporation would have a consistent product at numerous campus locations as well as offering 'home delivery' but would lose the artisan, local flavour that we believe adds diversity and creativity. The franchising of educational delivery will attempt to achieve consistency, but I am unsure if it will be either successful or desirable as student choice will be restricted to a few global brands.

The desire to be or to have a 'world-class university' is an aspiration that seems to be shared across the globe and is often one of the key messages in educational policies and institutional strategies. Looking from a global perspective, we can see that the delivery of higher education is becoming an increasingly crowded market, with suppliers emerging across the world.

In the UK we are resting on our 'brand identity' developed over decades and centuries but, if we sleep too deeply, we could overlook that students and academics are increasingly recognizing the growth of HEI sectors in countries we would never have considered as part of our peer group. Aspiring countries are taking the development of a higher education sector seriously as a long-term strategic decision to develop their economic and global standing. A recent World Bank study (Altbach and Salmi, 2011) explored the experience of 11 leading public and private research universities from Africa, Asia, Latin America and Eastern Europe. The study concluded that there are common characteristics for the top performers, without which 21st century universities cannot hope to survive, let alone excel:

- a high concentration of talented academics and students
- significant budgets
- strategic vision and leadership.

The optimist in me recognizes that two of these characteristics are within the gift of our own institutions: a high concentration of talented academics and students and strategic vision and leadership. So, for services in universities and the information professionals who work in them, there is a clear challenge: if we want to thrive, we must focus on the services and support which will facilitate an increased concentration of talented academics and students and we must actively contribute to the institution's strategic vision and leadership. Routes to achieve this lie in the excellence and relevance of our services to a global academic and student population. National or even regional trends for 'world-class services' should take a second place to international benchmarking to search for the best service solutions. When considering the question 'what do academics and/or students want?', accessing global research will be key; we are not playing to a national market, and our academics and students are mobile and will expect the best in class from India through to the USA in the services we provide.

However, there remains the final characteristic as defined by the World Bank study - significant budgets. These can no longer be achieved without a significant focus on collaboration. Making sure that your service and institution has a 'significant budget' is a more tricky (or even potentially an iniquitous) problem. In the UK we are seeing an increasing shift to student-financed teaching with the introduction of the fee regime, so we can argue that our teaching budgets lie within our sphere of influence. Conversely, the allocation of student numbers and commitments to particular aspects of government admissions policies (also explored in Chapter 5) means that the supply of students is regulated so that 'market forces' and our ability to react are restricted. Research income across the globe is highly publicly funded by nations, regions and global institutions. Even significant aspects of the availability of private funding relate to (often global) policy decisions, for example, policies to decrease carbon production result in manufacturing- and energy-industry-funded research to deliver innovations to help meet these targets. Accessing research income is increasingly a collaborative venture, so to achieve research funding success we need to be part of a group of, usually international, collaborative partners – and we need to be able to bring our international peers together at short notice in response to tight timescales in calls for funding.

The only route for success in securing a 'significant budget' is to ensure the concentration of talented academics and students via 'best-in-the-world services' and to have the strategic vision and leadership to deliver. Using collaboration we can develop 'best-in-world' services rapidly – exchanging knowledge and experience and exploiting opportunities to share services. We need high-level financial and budgeting skills to deliver savings, however, as budgets will not expand, and to negotiate almost always in collaboration with other institutions results in better prices for the services and resources we procure. Therefore a successful, collaboration-rich library and information service will:

- provide relevant, valued and world-class services, so that academics and students are not only attracted but also retained by our institution
- work to influence the strategic vision of the institution through strong professional leadership and to align local strategies to ensure the institution's vision and leadership is supported
- have high level skills in financial management and budgeting to negotiate collaboratively with suppliers and within their institutions to secure the best possible budgets for services – all focused on services to attract and retain academics and students in alignment with the university's strategy and leadership
- be able to group together, at short notice, a collaborative peer group for research income success.

From local to global: changes in knowledge access and exchange

The monopoly model we have been working within to deliver knowledge access and exchange is increasingly being challenged not only between universities but also outside our sectors' walls via technological innovations. The university on the far side of the globe is not our only competitor; it is also the access to information on desktop PCs and mobile devices and the creation of content using those same devices at any location across the globe. In the *The Edgeless University*, Bradwell explores the fact that universities are experiencing an edgeless sprawl:

> The function they perform is no longer contained within the campus, nor within the physically defined space of a particular institution, nor, sometimes, even in higher education institutions at all. This is driven by people finding new ways to access and use ideas and knowledge, by new networks of learning and innovation, and by collaborative research networks that span institutions and businesses. It is an increasingly international phenomenon. Across the globe, countries are pushing for greater advantages in education and innovation. There is an ever-growing environment of learning, research and knowledge exchange of which universities are one part.
>
> (Bradwell, 2009, 8)

So collaboration for knowledge exchange means working both within and outside our professional and institutional boundaries. We need to develop projects where we are part of a multi-service team, so collaborating with other services and academic departments within our universities and delivering information where we work in collaboration with groups outside our perceived sector walls.

As we embark into an edgeless environment, knowledge access, creation and exchange are being transformed through the use of technology. In this era key questions are being asked, which potentially undermine preconceptions and foundations of the HEI and its library services: 'Can't we just use Google?'; 'So why do we have a library (or even a university)?', and there is growing debate about the sustainability of the scholarly publishing model as highlighted by the publication in late June 2012 of the Finch Report (Finch, 2012) suggesting the tantalizing opportunity for the UK to become the first open-access nation. See also Chapter 7.

When I spoke recently to an alumnus who had attended Aberystwyth University in the 1960s, they stressed their gratitude on being allowed to enter the library, and regaled me with tales of the power of the librarian who could decide to help or hinder individuals in their quest for knowledge. The locked doors in our stacks have been prised open as the new methods for information access and exchange have created an environment where universities and their libraries no longer enjoy a monopoly on access to information:

> . . . the competitive market environment is the most significant change libraries face today. . . . Until the advent of the Internet, academic libraries had no competition and their patrons were a captive audience. Students and faculty either learned the protocols and organizational principles of the library . . . or did without. In today's environment simplicity, efficiency and transparency, combined with savvy marketing, have become critical factors in patrons' decisions in selecting information resources. Ease of access is often considered more important than quality. . . . Librarians must now confront disruptive innovation as a matter of routine.
>
> (Ross and Sennyey, 2008, 146)

There is a direct link in the disruptive innovations in access to information and in the creation of content. Try explaining to a taxpayer, unrelated to academia, why we expect them to pay at least twice for the same effort in salaries to the author and in subscription fees to the publisher, and all of this *for the same information*. Our complex reasoning on the quality, standards and reputational requirement for this 'pay twice to access the research' model cannot respond to such scrutiny.

There is also the issue of 'fairness' – the outputs from universities could only be accessed by other universities with the budgets to pay for the subscriptions. Most of the world's population would never be able to access the content because of cost.

I believe that most universities recognize that we have lost our 'access to information monopoly' – but we are not yet comfortably and routinely 'confronting disruptive innovation' (Ross and Sennyey, 2008, 146). Our first gentle attempts to recognize our loss of control resulted in huge efforts to create 'helpful links' pages and we catalogued web pages in a Sisyphean attempt to replicate the safety of our shelves in a digital environment. We have looked, mainly, to commercial suppliers to innovate and replicate the 'simplicity, efficiency and transparency, combined with savvy marketing' (2008, 146) of Google for our card catalogues, but our marketing efforts are a little less savvy than multinationals' so real competition is challenging, to say the least.

Any prediction in print format on the future changes in knowledge access and exchange will be out of date before the cover of the book has been selected. Nevertheless, I believe that open access will become the dominant route for publication; if reputation and quality are the last-resort arguments for the expensive pay-twice scholarly publishing model, then they will hold back open access as successfully as reading in the bath was expected to prevent the growth of e-books. Reputation will still be important (as will be reading in the bath) but we cannot hold back the genuine, common sense momentum that open access is gaining. Reputation will be delivered, just not at the cost of open access. Journals were created to allow knowledge exchange, which then progressed into opportunities for researchers to collaborate. We can be confident that the technological tools for open access publication in 2020 will have collaboration embedded from the moment of knowledge creation – even now an academic research blog on the use of library resources and the Twitter feeds of the researchers enable services, research projects and intuitions to collaborate from the earliest stages of the research, as suggested in Chapter 7. In my view, the certainty of the dominance of open access has one caveat – the technological tools used for open access publication in 2020 will be wholly different from the tools used today.

How can universities and their library and information services become comfortable in confronting disruptive technologies, in this new edgeless era? Guthrie and Housewright suggested evolution was needed:

> As faculty research and teaching practices continue to shift in response to their rapidly changing information environment, their uses of the library also change, as does their perception of the value the library offers. Faculty used to rely almost exclusively on the library for the scholarly materials they needed for research and teaching, and librarians guided faculty to and otherwise facilitated the discovery of these materials. As scholars have grown better able to reach needed materials directly online, going to or using the library is not essential to carrying out research and so faculty are turning to other options.
>
> (2010, 84)

It is important to note when advocating evolution that, while not backing one theory over any belief, adaptation takes generations (to simplify to the extreme: the giraffe's neck grew over time to reach the higher leaves) while mutation (a freakishly long-necked giraffe was born to standard, short-necked parents) is fraught with risks of swift natural selection but could potentially give a more rapid solution.

Hence, I would back the entrepreneurial librarian in an HEI who will remain committed to the concept of academic libraries as 'complex institutions with multiple roles and a host of related operations and services . . . '[whose] fundamental purpose has remained the same: to provide access to trustworthy, authoritative knowledge' Campbell (2006, 16). So the entrepreneurial librarian who will mutate services, risking failure, to push forward innovations will eventually succeed in exploiting disruptive technologies. Therefore a successful, collaboration-rich library and information service will:

- be part of the shift to open-access scholarly communication
- be entrepreneurial and mutate services, take risks, and learn from (regular) failures to confront disruptive technologies
- collaborate within and outside our professional and institutional boundaries, working as part of multi-service teams and with organizations and businesses outside our perceived sector walls.

From student experience to student expectation

In an earlier section, I described a 1960s alumnus telling me how grateful they felt to be allowed to use the library at Aberystwyth, and as a student I can recall my genuine feeling of being excited to be 'allowed' to attend. On reflection, both I and the alumnus are stereotypes – we left school, and university formed the bridge to our start in 'life'. There was a perception that the student experience was a journey for our generation and demographic. We were here to learn and to learn how to live, and if lecturers and librarians were wonderful that was nice but, if they weren't, we would tolerate it and make little comment during any staff-student consultative committees.

In the UK, the introduction of loans, fees and I predict the soon-to-be-introduced 'Compare my course.com' mashed from the KIS (Key Information Sets) has converted grateful experience to firm expectation. The KIS web pages, published by government funding council requirement in the UK from late 2012 (www.hefce.ac.uk/whatwedo/lt/publicinfo/kis), will allow students, parents and competitors to view metrics about each degree course, from student satisfaction ratings through to employment levels of graduates and teaching contact hours.

The expectations of the pre-'loans, fees and comparison site' students were low and the demographic was, for some, largely homogenous; they were 18, studying full time and they lived on campus. Delivering a student experience for a relatively uniform demographic with low expectations meant that course structures, pedagogic techniques and services to support learning and living could be delivered with relative ease and take little notice of the student voice as one size almost always fitted all. For the post-'loans, fees and comparison site' students this is not the case – they are a diverse community by age, gender, nationality and mode of study. One size *cannot* fit all. Now our reality is that diverse students are our customers. This creates a complex transactional relationship fraught with high expectations – and when we try to plan for the future to meet expectations with our services, we are trying to do that for individuals who we do not even know yet.

In the 2011 Annual Higher Education Policy Institute (HEPI) Lecture, Dr Jamil Salmi describes an encounter, for illustration purposes, where he asked a passerby about the future of higher education and the kinds of expectations that we could (shortly) be trying to meet:

> In the future, it will be compulsory to go to university. . . . Students will take open internet exams and the validity of their degree will be only five years . . . no more physical libraries or labs; it will be all i-labs and e-libraries . . . if [graduates] don't find a proper job within six months, you will have to reimburse them the costs of their studies.
>
> (Salmi, 2011, 1)

If this is the future then we are already experiencing increasing expectations in the present. One of my favourite moments during recent student induction events was one student who was sitting on her rucksack, with all of her belongings on the floor beside her, intent on setting up her computer access account for the five different devices she intended to use. When I asked if she wanted to get to her accommodation and to sort out her luggage first, she exclaimed, 'It's more important to get the internet than a bedroom.' This might be an extreme example, but it demonstrates the shifts in living and learning expectations. Library and information services are part of people's lives - and this is a responsibility that we can't take lightly. I recognize that students and academic colleagues have incredibly high expectations of services - when they see a news report on a new technology they think this is a promise and that it will be available on their laptop in the morning. We can only understand student expectations by listening to students - not as feedback but as part of the service development process.

For the future, delivering the right technology will be as important as providing effective study spaces, and you can't do one without the other in our edgeless environment. Therefore a successful, collaboration-rich library and information service will:

- recognize that our students are customers with strong, diverse and even competing expectations, which rapidly change
- develop services through collaboration with students.

Never mind the quality, look at our rank: the influence of the league table

In a globally competitive market where our market segment has become edgeless and our customer expectations are rapidly changing, the prospective student, our governments, the funders, our competitors and the press have focused on league tables as a measure of rank, value and success. Metrics are mashed and world rankings are formulated – high scores are proclaimed by 'successful' institutions on marketing materials. Rankings have meaning for our reputation and increasingly our income. As noted by Li, Shankar and Tang (2011, 923), 'league tables increasingly have real resource implications for universities. This is because, despite the criticisms of their accuracy, reliability and usefulness, university rankings have been quickly adopted as a quality assurance mechanism around the world.' Evidence suggests that international students are increasingly using league tables to make decisions on where to study (Hazelkorn, 2008; HEFCE, 2008).

Criticism of league tables focuses on their perceived subjectivism, what they don't measure and the attempt to compare unlike with unlike. David Watson (2012, 6) described the narrow elements which count in the league tables as including research, graduate destination, infrastructure and international recruitment. Aspects which had little, or no, influence on league table scores included social mobility, collaboration and services to business and the community.

On one level it is tempting to channel energies on improving aspects of our universities that influence the scores, without a real or sustainable strategy for improvement. Working to exceed targets to leap up the league tables has led to some interesting ways of working in the National Health Service, where targets were met and performance was assessed as 'improved', but patient care suffered. As league tables measure such limited elements of a flourishing university then I am content to predict the failure of an institution where strategy and energy is focused solely in these narrow areas.

Students are also creating their own league tables and measures of success using social media tools (e.g. www.ratemyprofessors.com) so there are some real opportunities for us to collaborate to address the league table deficits indicated by Watson (2012). Why should universities rely on recognized flawed processes to define their success? Openly publishing our own rich content that we have created to help measure and enhance our performance, our internal metrics and key performance indicators (KPIs) will add definition and context to the broad-brush (and thus limited) view given by the league tables and social media sites. So, given that league tables will not reflect all of an institution's strategy or delivery, internal KPIs that flow from the strategy keep an institution grounded, allowing it to learn from the league table scores/social media, and consider ways to improve, while keeping the KPIs at the core of institutional performance measurement. If we work collaboratively on openly published performance information we can create our own valid and vibrant league tables, recognizing the opportunities for 'benchlearning', a way to share knowledge *and* experience, rather than just benchmarking using metrics as an indicator of success, as suggested by the European Commission (see www.epractice.eu/community/benchlearning). Therefore a successful, collaboration rich library and information service will:

- celebrate KPI successes and positive social media feedback with as much effort as the league tables and create its own media hype
- learn the lessons from KPIs, negative social media feedback and league table rankings to identify where improvements can be made but recalibrate their importance against its strong strategic plan
- collaborate through the open publication on our measures of success to create relevant and vibrant opportunities for rapid improvements through following best practice.

Conclusions – some options for future success

In our edgeless world we compete with multinational corporations, individuals using social media and other universities, based anywhere in the world. No single service or individual can come up with the solutions and innovations needed. The benefits of shared services, one of the deepest forms of collaboration, have been described in the JISC toolkit on Shared Services (2009) as including: continuity and resilience of service, raised quality and added value to existing services, secured cost savings and sustainable efficiencies, staff time made available for more customer facing activities, improvements to the scalability of systems, ensuring improved and more up-to-date systems, gaining competitive advantage and lastly the ability to offer otherwise unsustainable services.

These benefits can be easily translated as applying to all levels of collaboration – which at its simplest level would be knowledge exchange across our peer groups – so the ability to collaborate by emailing a discussion list or posting a conundrum on a blog and receiving answers from our international colleagues can all help achieve benefits where alone, in our complex edgeless world, we would struggle or fail.

There are some significant and exciting options as to how higher education can respond to the changing and challenging environments ahead. Governments, media and corporations have high expectations of how universities will rise to these challenges, for example as Eric Schmidt, the CEO of Google, said, 'we are going to have to innovate our way out of this thing [the economic crisis] and our great universities will have to lead the way' (cited in Thorp and Goldstein, 2010, 1). As reiterated previously, in the future universities will service, enable and deliver teaching, learning and research for students and academics who they don't yet know (so can't understand). They will want to use technologies that have not yet been developed, and will work under policies and governments not yet formed.

In this chapter I have touched on four main environmental factors: emerging globalization, the edgeless nature of knowledge access and exchange, the transformation of the student from experience to expectation, and the influence of league tables. In each of these areas I have offered some options for future success and how library and information services can become fit for the future, with a focus on collaboration as a catalyst for rapid change. The changing higher education context will mean that we need to mutate or face potential natural selection and/or extinction. I am confident that we have the ingredients, through collaboration, in our shared, talented staff and knowledgeable students to succeed. Creative and entrepreneurial working across services will be required to exploit our global and edgeless environment. We are competing locally, nationally and internationally with other universities and other sectors. If we plot our course and continue our journey together by focusing on a long term, clear strategic direction we can traverse the difficult paths to success.

References

Altbach, P. G. and Salmi, J. (eds) (2011) *The Road to Academic Excellence: the making of world-class research universities*, Directions in Human Development 64668, The World Bank.

Bradwell, P. (2009) *The Edgeless University: why higher education must embrace technology*, Demos, http://demos.co.uk/publications/the-edgeless-university.

Bruce, T. (2012) *Universities and Constitutional Change in the UK: the impact of devolution on the higher education sector*, Higher Education Policy Institute.

Campbell, J. D. (2006) Changing a Cultural Icon: the academic library as a virtual destination, *EDUCAUSE Review* **41** (1), January, 16-30, http://net.educause.edu/ir/library/pdf/erm0610.pdf.

Finch, J. (2012) *Accessibility, Sustainability, Excellence: how to expand access to research publications*, Report of the Working Group on Expanding Access to Published Research Findings, Research Information Network.

Guthrie, K. and Housewright, R. (2010) Repackaging the Library: what do faculty think? In Climbing Out of the Box: repackaging libraries for survival, special issue, *Journal of Library Administration*, **51** (1), 77-104, www.tandfonline.com/doi/full/10.1080/01930826.2011.531643.

Hazelkorn, E. (2008) Learning to Live with League Tables and Ranking: the experience of institutional leaders, *Higher Education Policy*, **21** (2), 193-215.

Herzfeld, A. (2005) *Revolution in the Valley: the insanely great story of how the Mac was made*, O'Reilly Media.

Higher Education Funding Council for England (HEFCE) (2008) *Counting What Is Measured or Measuring What Counts? League tables and their impact on higher education institutions in England*, HEFCE.

Joint Information Systems Committee (JISC) Infonet (2009) Shared Services Toolkit, www.jiscinfonet.ac.uk/infokits/shared-services.

Lewis, M. L., Davies R., Jenkins, D. and Tait, M. I. (2001) A Review of Evaluative Studies of Computer-Based Learning in Nursing Education, *Nurse Education Today*, **21** (1), January, 26-37.

Li, M., Shankar, S. and Tang K. K. (2011) Why Does the USA Dominate University League Tables? *Studies in Higher Education*, **36** (8), 923-37.

Ross, L. and Sennyey, P. (2008) The Library is Dead, Long Live the Library! The practice of academic librarianship and the digital revolution, *The Journal of Academic Librarianship*, **34** (2), 145-52.

Salmi, J. (2011) *Flourish or Fail? Higher Education in crisis – the global context*, Annual Lecture, Higher Education Policy Institute.

Thorp, H. and Goldstein, B. (2010) *Engines of Innovation: the entrepreneurial university in the twenty first century*, University of North Carolina Press.

Watson, D. (2009) *The Question of Morale: managing happiness and unhappiness in university life*, Open University Press.

Watson, D. (2012) *Misunderstanding Modern Higher Education: eight 'category mistakes'*, Higher Education Policy Institute, www.hepi.ac.uk/455/Publications.html.

2 Connecting with the student perspective

Craig Gaskell, University of Hull, UK

Acknowledgements

The work of Kate Dickinson (Scarborough HR Co-ordinator) and Howard Foster (Scarborough Student Experience Manager) is acknowledged in contributing to the themes of this chapter.

Introduction

Motivated by student feedback, we realized that our model of service delivery on the Scarborough Campus of the University of Hull could be improved, particularly from a student interface perspective. The existing approach suited the university looking from its structures outwards rather than the students looking in. A review took place with a critical look at the support functions, team structures and interface points both within academic departments and professional service areas on campus. The aim was to make things work better from a student viewpoint. The review recommended a radical restructure of campus administration and support functions, development of a new highly streamlined approach to student interaction and a redesign of the spaces critical to this activity. It yielded a new library and reset it as the focal point of interaction with students at the heart of the campus. This chapter describes the fundamental shift in approach at Scarborough and reflects on the impact two years on from starting the change process.

One-stop shops, service convergence and libraries

Schultz and Szekeres (2008) highlight provision of service at the right point in the organization as one of the key challenges for universities. Many institutions have developed the concept of the 'one-stop shop' to consolidate aspects of on-campus service delivery at the interface level. This is widely acknowledged to be a good thing from a student support perspective, with positive implications for improved student access (Universities UK, 2002) as well as improved opportunities for student-centred business improvements (Soderstrom and Hedestig, 2008).

Some universities have developed an *information commons* as a means of helping students manage information or extended this further in the spirit of a *learning commons* to bridge the gap between academic and professional services via a range of functions to support learning (Schmidt and Kaufman, 2007). In many institutions the converged services agenda has focused around the library, and the term *super-convergence* has started to gain currency as a way of describing this change, to capture the direction of travel (Appleton, 2010; 2011; Weaver, 2010; Bulpitt, 2012). Super-convergence is defined as: 'Bring[ing] together a range of support activities that are generally focussed on student support and are structurally converged in order to streamline provision' (Heseltine et al., 2009).

When we launched our review process back in November 2009, in addition to looking internally we started to look at what other institutions were doing in service convergence and library development, and as part of the process we visited colleagues at Liverpool John Moores University. Their experience of developing learning resource centres and the change processes they had undertaken were of particular interest (Appleton, 2010). Our project fitted with the spirit of super-convergence; however, we were looking to go further by encompassing all academic departmental administration as well as central services provision.

The Scarborough context

The Scarborough Campus is a 'satellite' of the University of Hull, located on the Yorkshire coast overlooking the town of Scarborough, 45 miles away from the main site of the university. Universities with multi-campus arrangements are common and we have recently undertaken a study of satellites within the UK, looking at strategic, structural and operational issues on the academic and service side (Gaskell, 2011). Schulz and Szekeres (2008) note that institutions with multiple campuses have additional levels of complexity in providing services to students; however, the smaller scale of satellite sites also provides opportunities for developing a joined-up approach.

Scarborough Campus is home to around 13% of Hull's students (almost 2000 full-time equivalent). The academic governance of the university is via a faculty structure, which spans the two campuses. The Scarborough Campus is not a separate faculty but is home to five academic units (departments, schools and centres), each from different faculties.

The Scarborough School of Education, a significant component of the Faculty of Education, is the largest department, focusing on initial teacher education for the primary phase together with a broader educational studies curriculum. The School of Arts and New Media, which includes subject provision in Digital Media, Music Technology, Theatre and English, is a department within the Faculty of Arts. The Centre for Environmental and Marine Sciences specializes in terrestrial and marine field-based science. It is a centre within the department of Biological Sciences, which is part of the Faculty of Science. Scarborough Management Centre is a subject grouping that is part of the Business School and provides a suite of business and management programmes. There is also a Centre for Employability and Professional Skills, which provides most of the part-time and short-course provision on campus and also delivers degree-level programmes, predominantly in the health and social care domain.

The full range of professional services and support activities is provided at the campus including library, IT, facilities (estates, catering, security and household), accommodation, student support, study support, registry, careers, etc. The prevailing structure has evolved to one of small locally managed teams, but with professional links back to the relevant Hull-based directorates.

Prior to the restructure described here, each academic department had its own administration teams covering a range of functions focused entirely on that department. There was a separate central team that encompassed central (registry-related) administrative activities. There were also staff with administration responsibilities working within some of the service areas.

The Students' Union (HUU) has an elected sabbatical officer, a Scarborough-based Vice-President, who is responsible for a small team of student volunteer officers based at Scarborough, as part of the Hull University Union structure. There is a full-time HUU-Scarborough manager and the HUU advice centre also provides some support in situ for Scarborough Campus students.

Motivation to change

From a top-down faculty-oriented viewpoint the structure in place made complete sense. However, we started to get indications through various student feedback mechanisms on campus that this wasn't necessarily the case when looking at the organization through the eyes of the students. The Scarborough Campus context meant that we had students from several different faculties studying different programmes but all within the same compact campus environment and all using the same general facilities. Hence any sense of inconsistency in different faculty approaches was much clearer to see in Scarborough than at the larger Hull campus, where departments from the same faculty tend to be grouped together.

We therefore launched a review of administration and support in Scarborough.

Our focus was to examine the current administrative and support roles on campus, making an appraisal of the central and departmental support that was in place, looking at both the academic and service areas. The review progressed in stages and covered student administration services (registry-type functions), facilities, campus reception and postal services, learning resources (library and IT), student support services, finance support and the administration elements of the School of Arts and New Media, Scarborough School of Education, Centre for Environmental and Marine Sciences and Centre for Employability and Professional Skills. The Scarborough Management Centre was only partially included because of their concerns at the time that any restructure away from a purely faculty-oriented model might compromise their professional accreditations. The aim of the review was to develop a model for the future of support (academic and service) at Scarborough that would ensure an effective, efficient and robust approach, with specific attention focused on student-facing aspects.

Conversation-based review process

A small review team was established comprising the University Registrar and Secretary, human resources (HR) colleagues (one based in Hull, the other based in Scarborough) plus the Principal of the Scarborough campus. The two Scarborough-based staff led the review and stakeholder engagement on both Scarborough and Hull campuses. The broader review team acted as a check and balance for the process and ensured a wider institutional perspective was considered, meeting as a group on eight occasions and keeping in regular contact throughout.

We started from the premise that a closed review approach, which lacked significant engagement of the primary stakeholders, would ignore the perspectives of those most closely involved and with whom the long-term success or failure of the change would rest. Jim Grieves (2010) discusses change-resistance and notes that resistance can occur when senior managers act as 'naive agents of change' or are 'seeking politically expedient motives for short-term gain'. We were determined not to fall into this trap and so committed to a process of extensive engagement, focused around conversations with all individuals involved (Shaw, 2002; Munn, 2007).

Another principle adopted was to ensure separation between the logical and physical aspects to enable work on the essence of the change, unconstrained by the details of current practice, current structures and the current physical environment. To enable this we went through the following four-step process, inspired by classical software systems analysis (DeMarco, 1978):

- Step 1: Analyse the *current physical* configuration (how are we doing things now?)
- Step 2: Understand the *current logical* approach (what are we currently doing?)
- Step 3: Develop a *new logical* approach (what should we be doing?)
- Step 4: Develop a *new physical* configuration (how should we do it?).

Our conversations with individual colleagues started soon after launch of the review. Prior to each meeting, colleagues were asked to complete a short questionnaire. In addition to providing a tool to capture information, this also acted as a vehicle by which colleagues could prepare for the discussion. The meetings were flexible and informal in nature, rather than highly structured; however, the questionnaires provided useful background information and cues for the discussion.

Colleagues were surprisingly open and frank, willing to share details of their individual roles and responsibilities, critically reflective of their own practice and candid about what they felt worked and what didn't. They were also very open about workload issues and in addition to identifying workload peak times they also indicated troughs, which were highlighted as equally problematic. Individual and distributed team workload fluctuations emerged as a key theme and we followed this up with a more detailed analysis where individuals provided an estimate of their workload peaks and troughs, month by month, over the course of a full academic year. We also encouraged individuals to reflect on their personal skills and aspirations. A side effect of the process was a much deeper understanding of the workforce.

This all took place with support of the current line managers (who were either local academic- or service-department heads). These colleagues, whom we termed the leaders group, had management responsibility for the individuals engaging in the review and it was critical that they were fully engaged in the project at all stages. The leaders group had to trust the integrity of the review, since at its core was direct and open engagement with their own staff. We worked with the leaders group separately and engaged them in facilitated meetings focused on taking a high-level view of the common good, removed from the current silos.

In addition to meetings with individuals we had regular feedback meetings with all participants in the review (to which the current line managers were invited) to play back our broad findings and our thinking as it was developing. We also engaged actively with institutional service heads based in Hull to ensure their views were taken account of. We also engaged with a student representatives' focus group and with the Students' Union.

The first stage of the review process involved around 100 meetings, most of which were with individuals, and 70 colleagues were engaged in total. The ensuing change process that followed the review impacted the roles of 40 administration staff directly and the broader direction of travel that was set in train would impact a much broader range of professional services roles subsequently. Our approach, which is documented in more detail elsewhere (Gaskell and Dickinson, 2011), involved looking outwards as well as inwards and was informed by available literature (Shaw, 2002; Munn, 2007; Kenward, 2008; Grieves, 2010) and current practice (Appleton 2010).

Review outcomes

Despite the indication of a highly committed group of professional services and academic departmental administration staff we found a number of issues to be addressed in our current fragmented approach to administration and service support provision. These included the following:

1 *Inconsistency*: Even making allowances for different subject cultures, there were arbitrary differences in academic departmental administration processes and no sense of consistency across the campus when viewed from a student perspective. Students from different faculties experienced variations in the way in which their respective faculties and departments were implementing university processes.
2 *Poor communications*: Academic departmental silos were not facilitating good cross-campus communication and practice sharing. There was a stark lack of communication between colleagues doing fundamentally similar roles in different academic departments. Some had never even met each other, let alone discussed practice sharing, despite all working on the same, compact campus.
3 *Excessive interface points*: As anticipated, one very significant issue was the student interface, the symptoms of which had been a primary driver for launching the review in the first place. There were 14 major student-interface points (including academic departmental offices, central administrative offices, and library and IT help desks) across a relatively small campus. Each had its own interaction culture, and each worked from the perspective of the particular organizational unit involved, with a general lack of global perspective. Despite the willingness of colleagues always to be helpful, the narrowness of knowledge in each office meant that students could end up being passed around the campus from office to office.
4 *Mixing interface and back office*: Individual staff often discharged both interface and back-office duties from the same, often shared, office

environment. Constrained office hours had been introduced for some interface tasks in an attempt to manage this and ensure time for the often confidential back-office work to be undertaken; however, that led to more limited interface availability.

5   *Overloaded roles*: In some cases staff worked in very small teams and by virtue of this some individuals had a broad range of responsibilities and a wide variety of different functions to perform. Transactional finance responsibilities, for example, were a small part of a number of colleagues' roles. Although staff clearly valued variety in their roles, there were significant knowledge, training and communication overheads, and in some cases institutional-compliance problems. Multi-role individuals were using different information systems for their various roles, but not necessarily on a regular enough basis to ensure fluency with particular systems. Related to this was the issue that many staff had student interaction as part of their broad roles but didn't see this as their primary professional role.

6   *Critical business risks*: There were several instances of sole individuals holding aspects of business-critical intelligence, leaving the university vulnerable to staff departures. Tight coupling of administrative staff to particular programmes, combined with small teams, also seemed to add an unnecessary inflexibility constraint for potential academic developments. We would often see business cases for new academic programmes accompanied by the need for a new part-time administration post to support them.

7   *Single points of failure*: The lack of knowledge-sharing between different specialist roles meant that staff absence could have a disproportionate impact on service level, including at the student interface. Providing cover from within the small teams was difficult, and never happened across teams because of the inconsistency of approach.

It was clear that although there was a structural logic to the approach from a faculty and departmental perspective, the service level was suboptimal from a student perspective. In addition the approach was also fundamentally inefficient, and career development and progression was limited for the staff involved.

Taking a fresh perspective

The findings of the review caused us fundamentally to rethink our approach to delivery of the professional services and organization of the administration on campus. We set aside the constraints of existing organizational structures and physical spaces, and went back to first principles. The new approach that emerged put the student perspective at the centre and categorized our supporting provision in terms of its proximity to direct student interaction. The essence of the new concept, the Onion Slice Model, includes:

- Layer 1: the *interface*, which represents functions that directly interact with students
- Layer 2: *academic support*, which represents functions that support the academic endeavours but don't involve direct engagement with students
- Layer 3: *corporate support*, which represents functions not directly related to the academic business; they are most distant from direct student interaction but are necessary to enable the corporate entity to function.

Having established the conceptual model we then considered all our administrative support and professional services provision in terms of *functional groupings* rather than using the vertical faculty or directorate-oriented groupings that were currently in place. If mapped onto the Onion Slice Model the current teams would span multiple layers.

The review recommended a new team structure that reorganized staff into campus-wide functional teams, providing a consolidated central student interface and grouping individual team activities around a single layer of the onion where possible. On the administration side all administrative activities from academic and professional service departments were grouped into three new teams, each sitting at a different layer of the onion slice.

At the heart of the concept was movement to a single consolidated student interface team that sits at Layer 1 of the onion. The new team, which we called *Campus Connect*, encompasses all previous student-facing first-line interface points on the academic and service side from around the campus, replacing all departmental offices and a variety of help desks. The Campus Connect team operates from a single point in the library. The next section discusses Campus Connect in more detail.

Sitting at Layer 2 of the onion, the *Student Administration* team was formed to deal with all aspects of academic-related administration including work done by the previous central administration team and all programme and student support functions previously undertaken by administrators in each of the separate academic departments. These staff (and roles) had been distributed across the campus, came under several different academic and service management lines, and operated from a host of different offices. All members of the new team were co-located into a single open-plan office. The team naturally split into two sub-teams, one dealing with programmes and the other dealing with central and registry-related administration functions, but all work closely together, enabling staffing resource to be optimized around priority tasks at different points in the academic cycle. The campus Student Administration and Quality Manager takes overall responsibility for this team.

A new *Corporate Support* team was created to consolidate all administration support functions that operate at Layer 3 of the onion slice. The functions carried out by this team include secretarial support for heads of department, financial processing support, transactional HR support, external-facing campus reception, telephony and copying services, facilities support and any other tasks that provide Scarborough-based colleagues (academic or service) with administration support that is not related to academic programmes. This team encompasses a host of activities previously undertaken by a range of colleagues in academic and service departments. Again we co-located team members as soon as the opportunity arose to create a single integrated team. The Corporate Support team reports through an office manager to the campus Finance and Business Manager. The campus HR co-ordinator is also located close to the team and has influence on it, although she doesn't have any formal management responsibility.

Campus Connect

The restructuring project was accompanied by a physical transformation of the campus focused around the Keith Donaldson Library. The new library spaces include silent study, social learning, group working, presentation rehearsal facilities, bookable meeting rooms, a coursework hand-in point, the careers service, the majority of open-access IT facilities and, of course, books and other learning resources that are all RFID-tagged so that they can be loaned and returned using the auto-checkout machines.

From the student perspective the most significant transformation that took place was the development of Campus Connect, the new consolidated first-line interface team. Operating from a desk in the social learning area of the library the Campus Connect team provides a single one-stop shop for all students to make any enquiry, raise an issue or concern, face to face, by telephone or via e-mail, along with an interface to all campus services and departments. The Campus Connect team is empowered to take personal ownership of each student enquiry and to see this right through to satisfactory resolution. Members of the team have been developed with a strong embedded service-delivery ethos. The Campus Connect desk is always staffed, but members of the team are also often out and about in the library, to help provide proactive support, looking for students who may need help and also observing behaviours that may inform further development of the space and services offered.

The Campus Connect team comprises a mixture of permanent employees supported by a casual pool of current and ex-students. This mix works well and the student employees provide valuable insights that ensure the student perspective is always in primary focus. The campus Student Experience Manager is responsible for the whole Campus Connect team, while day-to-day the operational supervision is provided by a group of student experience team leaders. The rest of the team comprises student experience assistants. Care needs to be taken around issues of confidentiality; student experience assistants who are also current students don't get full access to the complete information base that other team members get for student data confidentiality reasons. Data access control is handled very carefully.

The Student Experience Manager is a new role created as a result of the super-convergence. The role holder is a customer service professional, with a background from outside higher education and he has responsibility for measuring and facilitating improvement of all aspects of the student experience, but with a primary focus on the service side. Academic aspects are the primary responsibility of the academic community overseen by the campus Deputy Dean, who works closely with the Student Experience Manager. The Student Experience Manager chairs the campus Student Services Improvement Group and is also an active member of the University Student Services Executive Group, which is chaired by the University's Director of Student Services. The link between the University's Director of Student Services and the Scarborough campus Student Experience Manager is important both for practice sharing and to ensure alignment with broad university policies.

In addition to responsibility for Campus Connect, the Student Experience Manager also has overall responsibility for the library team and the student support team. He is managed directly by the Campus Principal and is part of the campus executive, which is a group of academic and service heads based at the campus. The Scarborough library team is managed directly by an academic liaison librarian who, in addition to her solid local management line, maintains a professional link to the University Librarian and broader library leadership team. This provides a model of local empowerment combined with appropriate institutional-level co-ordination and governance.

The Campus Connect team is available physically in the library from 7am until midnight on weekdays during term time, offering an extended service to students outside 'normal' office hours. This is a significant improvement in service from the previous model. If team members encounter an issue that cannot be resolved immediately, which can sometimes be the case for a detailed technical query that occurs late in the evening, they will arrange for the student to be contacted the next working day, at a time to suit them and by their preferred contact method. They will also ensure that the follow-up has occurred and the issue has been dealt with. Figure 2.1 shows a member of the Campus Connect team helping a student with a query.

Figure 2.1 *Campus Connect interaction*

The Campus Connect team use quieter periods to progress a range of initiatives that will improve the overall student experience, and it is anticipated that through proactive measures the day-to-day interactions at the desk will reduce. Online resources are in constant development to enable more self-help and remote access to information and support round the clock. The Pocket Campus website provides open access online information and is being developed as an electronic manifestation of Campus Connect. Pocket Campus is available via the web so that students can access the information anywhere and it is also available on campus via a number of touch-screen information points. When students approach the Campus Connect team requesting information that is available on Pocket Campus, they will be shown where this is so that they can access it online in future if they wish. However, we anticipate some students will always prefer face-to-face contact, even for library book loan and return transactions.

The ever-increasing knowledge base of the Campus Connect team results in more and more enquiries being satisfied at the first point of contact. If the answer isn't to hand, or is outside the team member's area of expertise, then they find it out or arrange for someone to contact the student. In order for this knowledge to be consolidated and shared across the team the staff are constantly developing an online information base of questions, answers and processes, which is for their own internal use. This activity is leading to much questioning of how we do things and an emergence of consistent practice.

A Campus Connect Student Charter has been developed that clearly states what students should expect from the team, with measurable service standards. Two-way service-level agreements are also being developed with other service and academic teams, incorporating key performance indicators and review meetings. Hence, under the leadership of the Student Experience Manager, the Campus Connect team not only provides a primary interface point for students but also provides a focal point for measurement and improvement of all student-facing services service on campus.

Reflections to date

At the point of writing we are approaching the end of the second year of operating in the super-converged configuration. We have just gone through a process of reviewing how the new library space is working for the students and have a number of improvements to implement; however, the overwhelming feedback from the student consultation events, which the Students' Union have taken a lead in organizing, has been extremely positive.

Campus Connect uses various mechanisms to encourage ongoing student feedback. The majority of comments have been very positive, with any negative feedback relating to specific issues such as an IT hardware failure or objection to paying library fines, rather than the Campus Connect service itself. Indeed we are consistently receiving very positive comments, such as those included below (which are typical):

'Extremely helpful, polite and dedicated to the job and my query.' - Year 2, Primary Teaching

'My request was handled very promptly and professionally and I was happy with the help I received. Thank you.' - Year 4, International Business

'Today the help desk lived up to its name. Thanks for all.'

'Was so helpful and friendly. Resolved my query very quickly to much satisfaction.'

'Great and friendly service. Everyone is fantastic.'

'Lady was extremely helpful in getting my laptop set up to the internet.'

'Excellent service as always. Library staff are always welcoming and helpful.'

The restructure has had a significant impact on the Scarborough Campus library team. Staff no longer sit at an issue desk since the Campus Connect team now deals with loans, returns, fines, etc. The library team members have a responsibility to ensure that Campus Connect is supported in delivering the first-line interface service; however, their energy is now much more directed towards adding value in their professional area. Maggie Sarjantson, our Academic Liaison Librarian and manager of the Scarborough library team, offered the following as a reflection on life two years into the change:

> Interestingly, I could write much more about opportunities and am rather struggling with the challenges. This is partly because we've already faced a variety of challenges over the last 2 years and have evolved into a very different team. We have self-evident levels of library staff engagement and motivation, and a sense that the team is empowered to drive change. Colleagues are involved in campus and university working groups and projects to a much greater extent than ever before, and are developing stronger relationships and networks. There's a lot of hard work ahead but also a genuine sense of excitement that the team can be more engaged in the educational rather than the purely procedural side of campus life.

The size of Maggie's team has actually reduced but its capacity has increased due to removal of the desk-based transactional duties. She reflects on this:

> It's interesting to consider the significant amount of time we've gained. If we think simply in terms of the full-time library assistants we now have fewer staff but have gained a whole person week every week. . . . This certainly generates heightened expectations of what we can now start to deliver.

One remaining challenge for the library team, which is very similar to that faced by the student administration team, relates to the staff now being less visible, and hence having less routine student contact. The team is working on a number of projects that will help raise the profile of the library service and of individual team members to both students and staff. These include improvement of reading lists and support for reading-list development, more direct interaction with student groups to enhance their use of the library and better facilitate the transition to

HE-level learning, initiatives to help remove 'library anxiety', and development of models to better support and embed digital literacy into the academic programmes.

The IT team IS experiencing a similar change, as Amanda Withey, our IT manager, explains:

> With significant progress being made with campus connect staff providing front line IT support, this has provided the IT team opportunity to move towards a different working model, and be proactive in making significant service improvements. The team are now in a position to dedicate more resource/time to project work which had previously received less focus. . . . Those members . . . who previously spent a regular amount of their working day on the Service Desk are now able to focus on more specialist IT functions.

On the student administration side we now have consistent processes across the different academic areas, and a consolidated group of individuals able to deal with queries or help progress student cases. Previously this fell to single individuals in each academic area. All academics across campus now receive a more consistent service.

The academic departmental heads, who have lost direct control of their administrators, also remain positive. One of the academic heads commented that the new approach provides:

> significantly easier access to a much broader range of administrative expertise and an apparently larger administrative resource.

Feedback from student course representatives has also been extremely positive. One course representative, who had raised initial concerns about losing their separate departmental office at the start of the process, has now expressed a preference for the new approach indicating that they are now able to 'go to one place where they seem to know everything'.

Although there is further work to do as the change beds down (and we are still in the process of seeking feedback from staff and students to enable further evolution), early indications are that the service levels have improved significantly.

Some of the support areas were initially reluctant to hand over all of their administration activities to the Corporate Support team; however, this is another example of a team where the net staffing numbers have reduced but the capacity and empowerment to be proactive has increased. The process of forming the Corporate Support team unearthed a number of inefficient working practices and some compliance issues, but these have been simple and quick to resolve.

The support staff base is now much more flexible and although there are primary leads for different academic areas within both Corporate Support and Student Administration, expertise is being shared and the single points of failure have been removed. Administrative colleagues are now in larger groupings, with a noticeable increase in team culture. Staff have adapted well to the large open-plan office environment, which has also improved our space utilization and equipment costs. The new larger team configuration and functional groupings provide colleagues with improved career opportunities with more visible routes for moving both sideways and upwards, and for engagement in projects.

One negative expressed by colleagues in the Student Administration team has been the loss of direct contact with students, and being considered 'back office' has been an issue for some, even though there is strong support for this being the right approach. This relates closely to the critical challenge faced by the library team losing their explicit front-of-house roles. As a result we are looking to provide more opportunities for these colleagues to get involved in student-facing activities, projects and events.

The primary driver for the review and ensuing super-convergence project was to improve the service from the perspective of the students. All evidence to date suggests that we are succeeding in that, although there is still more work to be done. However, there are also other significant benefits that have resulted, including a reduction in our operational baseline administrative staffing costs at Scarborough by over 10% within the first year of the change implementation. The structures that have been established will also enable further service improvements and efficiency gains in the future. Our experience supports Jack Kenward's assertion that 'the same number of support staff can do more together than they can do alone' (Kenward, 2008), and we would assert that service-level improvements, staff empowerment and efficiency gains go hand in hand.

References

Appleton, L. (2010) Living through Super-Convergence: creating library and student support at Liverpool John Moores University, *SCONUL Focus*, **49**, 67-70, www.sconul.ac.uk/publications/newsletter/49/22.pdf.

Appleton, L. (2011) Super-convergence. Liverpool John Moores University Conference Review, *SCONUL Focus*, **51**, 85-9, www.sconul.ac.uk/publications/newsletter/51/27.pdf.

Bulpitt, G. (ed) (2012) *Leading the Student Experience: super-convergence of organisation, structure and business processes*, Series 3, Publication 5, Leadership Foundation for Higher Education.

DeMarco, T. (1978) *Structured Analysis and System Specification*, Yourdon Press.

Gaskell, C. (2011) *Understanding Satellite Campuses: a small development project funded by*

the Leadership Foundation for Higher Education. Final Report, Leadership Foundation
for Higher Education, www.lfhe.ac.uk/research/smallprojects/sdp2010projects.html.

Gaskell, C. and Dickinson, K. (2011) Engaging Change. In Perspectives: policy and practice
in Higher Education,
www.lfhe.ac.uk/en/research-resources/commissioned-projects/small-development-
projects/
sdp2010/hull-po.cfm.

Grieves, J. (2010) Organizational Change Themes and Issues, Oxford University Press.

Heseltine, R., Marsh, S., McKnight, S. and Melling, M. (2009) Super-Convergence:
SCONUL shared-experience meeting, 16 February 2009, SCONUL Focus, 46, 121–4.

Kenward, J. (2008) Is There a Best Way to Structure the Administration? Perspectives:
policy and practice in higher education, 12 (4), 103-9.

Munn, B. (2007) Conversational, Not Confrontational: a new approach to quality. In
Marshall, S. (ed.), Strategic Leadership of Change in Higher Education: what's new,
Routledge, 31-41.

Schmidt, N. and Kaufman, J. (2007) Learning Commons: bridging the academic and
student affairs divide to enhance learning across campus, Research Strategies, 20,
242-56.

Schulz, L. and Szekeres, J. (2008) Service Provision to Students: where the gown best
fits, Journal of Higher Education Policy and Management, 30 (3), 261-71.

Shaw, P. (2002) Changing Conversations in Organizations: a complexity approach to change,
Routledge.

Soderstrom, M. and Hedestig, U. (2008) One-Stop Shops as a Means for Student Centred
Strategic Development of Higher Education,
www.eadtu.nl/conference-2008/proceedings/USBM%20-%20Hedestig%20and
%20Soderstrom%20-%20Student%20Centered%20Models%20for%
20Strategic%20Development%20of%20Higher%20Education.pdf.

Universities UK (2002) Student Services: effective approaches to retaining students in higher
education,
www.universitiesuk.ac.uk/Publications/Documents/services.pdf.

Weaver, M. L. (2010) The Flexible Professional: a fusion of cultures to support learning
and teaching. In TICER digital libraries a la carte 2010, Module 3, Partners in Teaching
and Learning, 26-30 July 2010, University of Tilburg, Netherlands,
http://insight.cumbria.ac.uk/330/1/TICER_PaperFinal.pdf.

3 Working with professional associations

Andrew West, University of Sheffield, UK
Raegan Hiles, AMOSSHE, UK

Acknowledgements

Thanks are due to the representatives and members of professional associations (in the UK and overseas) who provided information and advice for this chapter.

Introduction

The distinct career path for a 'professional' higher education (HE) administrator is a relatively new development. However, the professional associations in the UK have a long history; the Association of University Administrators (AUA) celebrated its golden jubilee in 2011, SCONUL (the Society of College, National and University Libraries) is over 60 years old and AMOSSHE, The Student Services Organisation, turns 20 in 2012, with its predecessor organization tracing a history back nearly 40 years. Professional associations have a variety of identities including as formalized sector bodies, lobbying groups, informal networks and incorporated organizations and societies. Professional associations are normally funded through membership subscriptions and operate as non-profit organizations. They usually seek to further a particular profession and/or the interests of their own membership. In the context of this chapter we consider professional associations in their roles fostering professional practice, professional identity and professional development, the focus being 'individual commitment to, and membership of, a professional community' (Hallas in West, 2011, 3).

The professional association landscape has evolved at an accelerated pace in the last 20 years, with increasing numbers of organizations and a growing prominence across a range of sectors. The Professional Associations Research Network (PARN) has commented:

Professional occupations have increased substantially in the last two decades. Growth has taken place not only in the traditional professions, but also in new professions that have emerged as changes in the nature of commerce, the values of society and advances in technology demand new skills and new specialisms.

(PARN, 2012)

PARN estimates that there are over 400 professional associations in the UK. It is likely that this is an underestimation, with easily 50 representing career specialisms in UK HE alone. In just this chapter, we reference over 20 professional associations supporting the HE student experience.

The HE landscape has also evolved significantly in the last 20 years. This degree of sector change, incorporating changing policy-drivers impacting on institutional missions, rising service demands and student expectations, new sector entrants and an increasing role for the private sector, means that HE professionals are increasingly reliant on their professional associations to keep abreast of sector developments and to maintain their continuing professional development (CPD) and level of expertise. To meet this need, the HE professional association landscape has experienced a similar scale of shift. In the very recent past we have witnessed mergers such as the British Universities Finance Directors Group (BUFDG) and Association of University Procurement Officers (AUPO), some being disbanded, such as the National Bureau for Disabled Students, and new associations formed, such as the National Equal Opportunities Network (NEON).

This chapter focuses specifically on professional associations supporting the entire HE student experience. We examine the current array of professional groupings, including those in the area of libraries and information management, and look at the way in which the professional associations operate and collaborate to support students holistically. A case study approach is used, focusing on AMOSSHE, The Student Services Organisation. We then explore the example of how one higher education institution (HEI), the University of Sheffield, encourages and benefits from interacting with professional associations in the area of the student experience, before considering the potential future scenarios for this group of professional associations, drawing on a number of international exemplars, by way of contrast and comparison.

The professional association landscape in higher education

Libby Hackett, Director of University Alliance, has argued that 'HE professional services staff are the ones who truly understand what it means to provide the wider student experience' (2011, 5). It is this understanding that shapes the HE professional associations which are led by those staff. It is also the associations that articulate for professional practitioners what it means to be at the heart of the student experience, so supporting members to reflect on and develop that understanding in a mutual exchange of reflective practice. There is no single 'student experience' professional organization, but several reflect, first, the various stages of the student journey and, second, the range of specific student-facing services, activities and functions. As indicated by Figure 3.1, some professional associations adopt an overarching view of service provision, especially supporting senior staff to take a strategic lead in service development. These organizations are complemented by a multitude of function-specific groupings reflecting particular roles and skills. While it would be wrong to suggest that the organizations with a primarily strategic focus do not also address professional skills competencies,

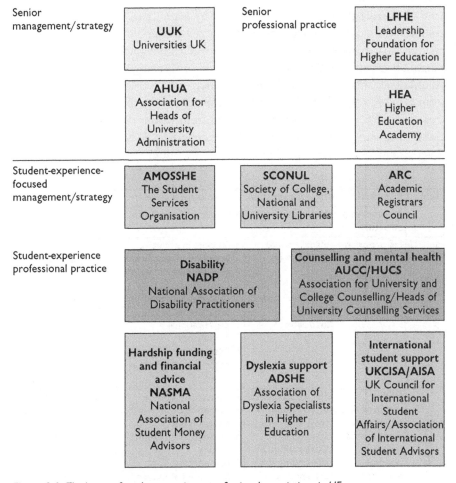

Figure 3.1 *The layers of student-experience professional associations in HE*

there is cross-membership across many of the groups, suggesting a degree of collaboration at the individual manager/practitioner level, which might not be immediately obvious, based on the existence of the apparently entirely separate organizations. Some reflections on how this varied landscape works out in practice in a specific HEI are included later in the chapter.

Figure 3.1 is illustrative rather than exhaustive. The specific service areas referred to are among the ten most frequently occurring responsibilities across UK HE student services teams (AMOSSHE, 2010).

Each of the professional associations is structured differently, with a variety of organizational models depending on history, approach to instruments like rules of incorporation and memoranda of association, as well as differing approaches to member input, reflecting distinct member needs. The overarching associations tend to operate their membership models by institution, with a set contact or contacts within that institution. Function-specific groups are more likely to involve an individual membership model. Income levels also vary across the associations, ranging from under £200,000 to over £1 million. Staffing structures range from voluntary arrangements to teams of 15 or more paid employees. All utilize some form of executive authority to direct the association – be that a board, council or trust – usually with elected representation from within the profession. And of course the membership 'offer' varies, depending on the focus of the organization. Some examples of this range of provision are set out in Table 3.1.

Table 3.1	*Professional association structure and membership benefits*			
	Membership structure	**Management**	**Member offer includes**	**CPD offer**
LFHE	HE providers	Elected board of 14 observers from HE agencies Core staff of 23 headcount and pool of associates	• Support individuals: leadership development programmes and events • Consultancy and coaching: in-house programmes and organizational consultancy • Research: exploring key challenges and changes in HE	• Training programmes and development centres, often residential • Networks and professional facilitation including Student Experience Network
AMOSSHE	HEI membership including up to three named members, optional additional members	Elected executive of 12 student services managers. Core staff of 2 FTE and pool of training facilitators	• Annual conference • Knowledge communities • National and regional groups • Networking • International exchange programme	• Residential annual conference • Minimum of five one-day training events, mixture of practical and strategic

Table 3.1 Continued				
	Membership structure	**Management**	**Member offer includes**	**CPD offer**
SCONUL	HEI and library membership	Elected executive board of 15 Core staff of 3 headcount	• Annual conference • Projects including impact initiative • Benchmarking • Expert groups	• Residential annual conference • One-day autumn conference • One-day events
Universities and Colleges Information Systems Association, UCISA	HEI, affiliate (sector bodies, overseas institutions), individual and corporate membership	Elected executive of 14 supplemented by 7 special interest groups Core staff of 7 headcount	• Annual management conference and two additional multi-day conferences • Specialist training courses • One-day events • Publications including toolkits, best practice guides, briefing papers and case studies	• Three residential conferences • Around 20 other events including development programmes run in collaboration with the LFHE and commercial trainers and themed one-day events
NASMA	Individual membership	Elected executive board of 12 Core staff of 1.7 FTE	• Annual conference • CPD programme • Projects including financial literacy research • Resources • Mailbase	• Residential annual conference • In-year training programme (18 one-day training events 2011–12) • Consultancy

Professional associations and the student experience: the case of AMOSSHE, The Student Services Organisation

A report by the Higher Education Funding Council for England (HEFCE) on financial sustainability concluded that the resources underpinning the student learning experience 'can be considered in three main parts: academic input . . . the learning environment . . . the student support services' (JM Consulting, 2008, 13). Professional associations are crucial in supporting staff to deliver these elements at the front line, in individual HEIs. AMOSSHE has argued that a 'distinctive feature of UK higher education is the personal interaction (what has been called the intimate relationship) between students and academic staff who are acknowledged experts in their field' (2009b, 2). This expectation extends beyond the traditional academic boundary into the domain of support, meaning that students expect financial advisors to be fully versed in the relevant elements of student funding; they expect careers advisors to be informed about the latest opportunities and attuned to best practice; and they expect qualified welfare support to be available on demand.

So while HEIs might be encouraged to put 'students at the heart of the system' (Department for Business, Innovation and Skills, 2011) or 'learners at the centre' (Scottish Government, 2011), such policy directives do not fully address the implications for professionals including matters such as adopting a more holistic approach to the student journey, demonstrating service excellence and improvement, and meeting associated CPD needs. It is the professional associations that address these issues – in the case of AMOSSHE across a full spectrum of service areas including widening participation, equality and diversity, student retention, money advice and financial services, counselling and student mental health, international student support, student induction and transitions support, employability, citizenship development, risk management, efficiency and cost effectiveness. With this in mind, AMOSSHE recently reviewed its purpose as a key professional organization at the heart of the HE student experience. This is embodied in the proposition that:

- AMOSSHE members shape the student experience in HE
- AMOSSHE empowers student service leaders
- AMOSSHE is a key voice of student experience leaders.

This positioning builds on the AMOSSHE strategy launched in 2010 alongside a restructured organizational base and a subsequently revised membership model. These developments have created a more effective association in business terms, and have led to increases in membership take-up and satisfaction (AMOSSHE, 2010, 2011a). AMOSSHE's member offer now includes a website containing a members-only resources area, CPD provision including one-day events and an annual residential conference, online activity including e-discussions, 'knowledge communities' operating as networks focused on specific service areas, quarterly member bulletins, policy briefings and associated lobbying activity, peer support and networking opportunities, regional activities, and project and developmental work. Over 75% of members value all of these items as very or fairly important within their membership (AMOSSHE, 2011a, 11); other less tangible but equally valued provision includes AMOSSHE's Executive and National Office's work to raise the profile of student services, AMOSSHE's contribution to policy discussions and their practical implications and AMOSSHE's role in articulating a professional identity for student services staff. AMOSSHE's political influence has increased alongside its strategic repositioning, more than doubling its level of engagement in national policy consultations and discussions since 2008. There is evidence of this impacting on subsequent policy developments: as an example almost all of the proposals AMOSSHE put to the Quality Assurance Agency (QAA) in 2011 concerning international student support were incorporated within the formally published guidance (AMOSSHE, 2011b; QAA, 2012).

Current collaborative initiatives

AMOSSHE's journey can be traced back to the developments in the HE sector referred to at the start of this chapter. Given the scale of change, it is perhaps not surprising that the various professional organizations supporting the student experience are increasingly working together in new ways. As the HE sector shifts, professional associations are embracing more collaborative approaches, not as an indication of deficit or weakness but in order to build strength and effectiveness. Some collaborations are evident in the area of business and administrative services, for example the co-location of the national offices of AUA and AHUA and ARC's contract with AUA, which involves the latter delivering administrative services for the former. There are increasing examples of a collaborative approach to member-CPD, such as a shared event on student mental health and well-being between AMOSSHE, AUCC and HUCS in 2010, and mutual involvement in national initiatives, such as AMOSSHE's support of NASMA's National Student Money Weeks in 2011 and 2012, and NASMA's support of AMOSSHE's Value and Impact Day in 2012. In addition to practical partnerships, collaborative approaches to governance are emerging, such as the AUA's consultative 'Council' of representatives of external stakeholder organizations, many of whom are other HE-sector professional associations, advising its Board of Trustees and converging around a President who represents the AUA in the external environment.

Other current examples of collaboration include joint policy-working such as AMOSSHE and ARC's combined contribution to debates concerning student finance (AMOSSHE and ARC, 2010) and high profile collaborative research and development projects. These are often funded through sector-wide vehicles like HEFCE's Leadership Governance and Management scheme. One key example is AMOSSHE's collaborative research project addressing the need for an evidence base to demonstrate the value and impact of student support services. While there was anecdotal evidence to suggest that student support makes a positive difference to the student experience, there was little solid evidence to support such statements (JM Consulting, 2008; AMOSSHE, 2009a, 2009b, 2011c). The Value and Impact Project advocated a move toward holistic evaluation of services and delivered a practical evaluation 'toolkit', which has been well received. The work was related to three key drivers and benefits:

- it underpins the evidence base for the contribution of student support services in HE – a particularly important theme when the HE student experience is perhaps in sharper focus than ever before;
- it forms part of the continued development of professionalism in the student services community and the increasingly strategic approach to the management and delivery of student service;
- it leads to demonstrable and practical improvements in the delivery of student services, so contributing to improved student learning, achievement and success.

(West in AMOSSHE, 2011c)

The development and governance of the Value and Impact Project was characterized by a strong commitment to the professional representative voice: sector professionals' personal commitment to contribute to models of practical support for the student experience profession. The project benefited from a practitioner-led peer support group, the members of which provided support and advice for the project as a whole, alongside buddying for those HEIs which piloted the emergent toolkit. Here we see an example of a professional association providing 'safe' space in which members can challenge established ideas and test new models, facilitating change in professional and management practice in a measured and co-ordinated way.

While the success of the Value and Impact Project was derived significantly from active practitioner engagement within the AMOSSHE community, the external sector-wide collaboration was also crucial. Potentially the project would not have secured funding without the range of other influential professional associations endorsing the original proposal. During the project, a number of important groupings including BUFDG, the Equality Challenge Unit (ECU), GuildHE, the HEA, the Joint Information Systems Committee (JISC) and UUK actively contributed to an overarching steering group. And at the point of project closure and dissemination, these organizations were at the heart of the work to endorse the toolkit within their own member communities, and to support further dissemination across the sector and beyond.

The influence of 'super-convergence'

In 2008, a group of SCONUL members identified a trend among some universities which were structurally drawing together new combinations of student-facing services, particularly libraries, technology and student services provision. This new service grouping, and its relevance to the professional associations, is discussed in Chapter 9 of this volume and thus we do not dwell on it here. Converging departments and functions and what is frequently referred to as 'restructuring' is of course a common feature of many organizations. What characterized this particular development in HEIs was the scale of convergence, hence SCONUL referring to 'super-convergence' and beginning a range of work to better understand the movement through shared experience networks and events (Heseltine et al., 2009). While a number of institutional drivers lie behind the super-convergence trend, it has also been driven to a significant extent by a focus on improving the student experience by providing more coherent and seamless support: students having 'their problems resolved in a single place' (Heseltine et al., 2009, 123).

As part of SCONUL's consideration of super-convergence, an initial tendency was noted 'for library and information professionals to talk (mainly) to other library and information professionals' (Heseltine et al., 2009, 122). Over time the discussion broadened, with a particular impetus stemming from the 2011 briefing to relevant professional associations from SCONUL and AMOSSHE (Melling, Selby and Hiles, 2011). This briefing paper specifically asked professional associations to consider their own role in super-convergence; the extent to which they already connected with or represented converged services; and whether they might support more formal networking opportunities and relationship building between the groups. Likewise, Bulpitt starts out by suggesting that staff's commitment to moving beyond the traditional bounds of their profession's core skills enabled super-convergence (2012, 5), but then goes on to grapple with the questions of leadership and skills expressed by Melling, Selby and Hiles (2011).

Professional associations have responded positively to the proposal to consider their role in supporting staff involved in super-convergence. Discussion is ongoing at the point of writing. Alongside this, the LFHE continues to develop a strand in its own work focused on holistic leadership in the student experience, including establishing a new network for relevant pro-vice-chancellors. The experience of those who have undergone super-convergence is that mutual learning has occurred across the 'partner' departments involved. In particular, broadening spheres of influence across a range of professional associations can better enable professionals to gather around shared goals and evaluation measures.

Professional associations in action: a case study from the University of Sheffield
Background

It may be helpful to illustrate some of these trends and developments as they have played out in practice within a particular HEI. The University of Sheffield is a large research-intensive institution with a wide spread of degree disciplines and more than 20% international students among the 25,000 enrolments. Student

Services is one of the largest of the University's professional service departments, with around 400 staff across a wide remit spanning the student 'journey' – from student recruitment, through admissions, registry, student administration, educational strategy and the associated quality management, student support and well-being and careers/employability. The department covers a very broad-ranging structure but does not incorporate library or IT services; these remain in separate departments, albeit with a number of strong operational links into Student Services. The strategic intent underpinning the University's Student Services structure is to better support the student lifecycle through taking account of the holistic student experience.

Operational approaches

A key practical manifestation of the integrated approach taken at the University of Sheffield is a front-line Student Services Information Desk (SSiD), which provides a 'one-stop-shop' function across the whole student journey, serving prospective students as well as current students and former students/graduates. This student-centric integration is popular with users and SSiD is consistently the best-rated university service for student satisfaction, as well as performing very strongly in external measures like i-Graduate's Student Barometer surveys. However, while the front-line service is integrated from a customer perspective, the one-stop shop overlays a rather complex organizational substructure made up of multiple functional teams based in numerous different locations and with significant variation in terms of professional identity and background.

Given the breadth of remit, Student Services at Sheffield includes colleagues holding sales and marketing roles, teams with a primary focus on process delivery and compliance matters (such as registry/student records), staff with a background in educational strategy and development, and services where ethical and well-being considerations are to the fore. This is in addition to a number of teams where there is a requirement for specific professional accreditation or the necessity for particular qualifications, such as in the area of health, chaplaincy and language support. Various attempts are made to foster a common identity across the teams and for the department as a whole. Collectively this is referred to as a 'better together' programme, which incorporates elements such as a common set of working values; a strategic approach to project working; cross-department communications; and a shared approach to issues like service monitoring and evaluation, staff development, staff well-being initiatives and the like. External review using the Investors in People standard (2012) suggests that these measures effectively support integrated working and a strong connection between strategy and operation.

Professional networking

The department is explicit in encouraging engagement in professional networks. Across the teams there are colleagues who are very active participants in professional associations including a number in regional or national representational and leadership roles. The organizations involved include those concerned with student recruitment such as the British Universities International Liaison Association (BUILA) and Higher Education Liaison Officers Association (HELOA); the ARC and its constituent practitioner groups in areas like admissions and student records; and educational/development/quality groupings like the Quality Strategy Network (QSN) and the Staff and Educational Development Association (SEDA). In addition, staff participate in a number of student support networks like NASMA, UKCISA, HUCS, the British Association of Healthcare Services for Students in Higher Education (BAHSHE) and the global forum for EAP (English for academic purposes) professionals (BALEAP), not to mention overarching organizations like AMOSSHE and the International Association of Student Affairs Services (IASAS).

When taken together this can be seen as an impressive array of development activity fostering professionalism, underpinning improvements in practice and ensuring appropriate validation in areas of legal or regulatory risk. The alternative view is that this is a proliferation of organizations representing an excessive overhead and a potentially over-complex or counterproductive professional model. In short, as fast as internal mechanisms attempt to encourage a common culture and a strategic user-centric view, a phalanx of professional bodies is (arguably) engaged in a rearguard action to preserve the distinctiveness of individual provider-centric domains, with additional spin-off groupings, specialist interest networks and new organizations emerging as the months go by. While that contrary viewpoint is probably a form of extreme caricature, it is certainly debatable whether the emerging connections between the professional associations (as entities) explored earlier in this chapter have any significant impact on the typical individual practitioner in a specific service area, still less at the front line, since many of the collaborations operate at an executive level or in the context of specific projects or developments.

As set out above, while AMOSSHE is one of the organizations with the greatest strategic reach across the student experience territory, its current membership model and groupings mean that the influence of any increasingly collaborative approach is likely to be much more limited within the more junior organizational layers, perhaps particularly in large institutions. None of this observation is intended to denigrate the vital contributions of professional associations in fostering professionalism, sharing best practice, and driving innovation and efficiency, but rather to suggest that the collaborative endeavours we have discussed might have a considerable distance to travel before they are fully embedded in every professional domain across the student experience.

The future
Questions

What conclusions can we draw from this brief overview of the current level of professional activity in student-facing services; what are the likely drivers for further collaboration; and what might the future hold for some of the fledgling collaborations and developing collaborative conversations referred to? Is there anything to learn from the experience of HE sectors outside the UK (in particular in the USA) where the professional landscape in the area of the student experience is probably more firmly established? We have seen that there is increasing evidence that a changing sector means evolving professional roles. Alongside the development of super-convergence, AMOSSHE's latest survey of members found that 'Student Services managers (now) deliver an even broader remit . . . continuing the (earlier) trend . . . of increasing responsibilities' (2011a, 2). At the same time there are suggestions that the new management challenges that sector trends present for managers include a potential emerging cadre of 'advanced generalist' staff (Melling, Selby and Hiles, 2011; Bulpitt, 2012). 'Advanced generalists' may originate from a variety of professional backgrounds, perhaps resulting in an enhanced need for professional association support.

Drivers for further collaboration

Building on this context, we might review the future development of professional associations in relation to three underlying 'drivers' towards further collaboration.

Student-centred services

First, the continued emphasis on what might be called student-centred services is observed in the trend towards super-convergence at some institutions and a focus on the holistic student experience, student lifecycle or student journey referred to in the case study from the University of Sheffield. It is reinforced by the context of rising student expectations referred to in the introductory part of this chapter and articulated in the work of organizations like the National Union of Students (NUS) and the former National Student Forum. While this driver raises implications for institutional service structures, we can also expect an increasing emphasis on collaboration across the professional groupings as managers look for support and innovation in terms of cross-cutting (strategic) functions rather more than in relation to individual specialisms. We might anticipate an increased demand for professional development in strategic areas like student mental health and emotional resilience, in addition to traditional CPD activity focused specifically on a function like counselling; and we might expect greater professional interest in a theme like student employability, rather than a narrower concern solely with careers services. We could see the further development of a professional theme like academic support, rather than a specific concern with information literacy; and we might see an increasing emphasis on a cross-cutting concept like customer service evidenced in Bulpitt's case studies (2012), running alongside a continuing interest in function-specific CPD.

Economic issues

UUK's work on efficiency, flexibility and adaptability in the HE sector pointed to the implications of significant change in the sector's funding arrangements (UUK, 2011, 4). This changing environment is just as relevant for the work of professional organizations and we may see economic conditions forcing a direction of travel towards mergers and collaborations if harder questions are asked about the value arising from involvement in many separate organizations, and the extent of overhead or duplication. The recent case of discussions leading towards a potential 'consolidation' of the two large, separate student affairs organizations in the USA (ACPA and NASPA) is instructive. While an extensive series of negotiations over a period of many months came to a end without any agreement to consolidate, a joint statement from the presidents of the two organizations stated positively that 'it is our intention to lead each association with its respective visions, *while at the same time, continue to encourage and support our ongoing collaborative effort*' (our emphasis, NASPA and ACPA, 2011). In short, the proposals for organizational consolidation had been laid to rest, but the future was mapped out strongly in terms of developing collaboration.

Business complexity

Contemporary management and leadership theories point to an ever-increasing complexity and interdependence in every organizational and business sector, implying the need for a different approach to leadership - moving from a focus on managing and protecting boundaries to what Yip, Ernst and Campbell (2011) have referred to as boundary spanning - the capability of managers to create direction, alignment and commitment across organizational boundaries in support of a broader, more strategic vision. Other writers have spoken of a 'hyper-connected' business world in which formerly 'complicated' environments are now significantly 'complex', containing multiple diverse but interdependent elements (Sargut and Gunther-McGrath, 2011). If, as argued in this chapter, a trend of increasing complexity is also evident in the context of HE, the professional manager's role becomes ever more demanding and there is an even more critical need for flexible leadership working across organizational boundaries, and collaborative activity to support individual professional career development and to underpin institutional success.

Collaborative working

Of course collaborative working falls into a spectrum of categories, depending on the range, extent, depth and impact of collaboration. The work of Keast, Brown and Mandell (2007) on the 'three Cs' of integration – co-operation, co-ordination and collaboration – is perhaps a helpful way to conclude these reflections as we look to the future. Within the terms of Keast et al."s model, 'co-operative' collaboration is characterized by activities such as information sharing and relatively infrequent communication, with a strong emphasis on the continued organizational autonomy of the various and separate stakeholders. A forum like the AUA Council mentioned above might perhaps fall into this category. Internationally, the recent development of a new overarching global organization for professionals involved in the field of student affairs (IASAS) represents a similar development. At present IASAS is an embryonic organization with a voluntary ethos and a degree of informality; over time this could be expected to develop into a more established and 'deeper' set of organizational and structural collaborations. Another example outside the direct focus of this volume but instructive nonetheless might be the UK Higher Education Senior Managers Forum, which operates as a round-table discussion group: 'a means for the main representative professional groups in the sector to collaborate effectively in areas where there are issues of shared interest' (AUDE, 2012).

Moving beyond the first C, 'co-ordinative' collaboration implies a more structured approach to communication flows – collaboration in the context of joint project-working, perhaps including shared project resourcing over a defined period but probably set in the context of a longer-term collaborative vision. Initiatives like AMOSSHE's Value and Impact Project exemplify this model, and it is a very well-established approach to project working within the student affairs community in the USA, with numerous examples of different organizations taking the lead role within a 'co-ordinative' setting, depending on the project area or the focus of research. A highly inclusive US initiative relating to the role of HEIs in supporting democratic action (arising from the work of a National Task Force on Civic Learning and Democratic Engagement) is a strong recent example from the American HE sector, with leadership stemming from the Association of American

Colleges and Universities and an array of related organizations and agencies actively involved in the project, including student-focused professional associations like NASPA.

Keast, Brown and Mandell's third C implies a maturity and depth of collaborative activity which is likely to be characterized by an explicitly collaborative strategic intent, collective decision-making, pooled resourcing and a long-term commitment to partnership working. The administrative 'shared services' relationship between ARC and AUA mentioned above could be seen to represent a successful example of this approach in the UK. In the US context, NASPA collaborates with a number of other cognate organizations to fund a shared staff post focused on governmental lobbying and policy analysis. NASPA also collaborates within a number of well established shared service operations, supporting functions like research, evaluation and benchmarking in their Assessment and Knowledge Consortium, and career and placement services for young professionals in their Placement Exchange, a partnership between NASPA and five other professional associations. Some of these initiatives also involve the direct involvement of private-sector partners.

Conclusions

The HE context continues to evolve and the development of the associated professional groups reflects that changing environment – trends closely tracked by organizations like PARN. As the HE sector, and within it the student experience 'territory', becomes more complex, universities and colleges are attempting to respond more holistically and strategically and there is emergent evidence of collaboration across the professional domains. Given the drivers for shared working, the focus on the student experience and the increasing commitment of professional associations to the collaborative agenda, it seems certain that the trends we have discussed will continue to develop. Ultimately the extent of effective collaboration achieved will depend on a creative combination of personal commitment from individual professionals in the sector, institutional aspirations regarding the student experience, and a supportive influence from the professional associations.

References

AMOSSHE (2009a) *Assessing the Value and Impact of Services that Support Students*, Funding Application to the Leadership Management and Governance Fund.

AMOSSHE (2009b) *Supplement to the HEFCE (FSSG) Report 'The Sustainability of Learning and Teaching in English Higher Education'*,

www.amosshe.org.uk/amosshe/assets/_managed/editor/File/AMOSSHE%20supple
mentary%20paper%20to%20the%200HEFCE%200FSSG%20Report%20Feb%
202009.pdf.

AMOSSHE (2010) *AMOSSHE Members' Survey 2009–10: the outcome* (members-only
resource).

AMOSSHE (2011a) *AMOSSHE Members' Survey 2010–11: the outcome* (members-only
resource).

AMOSSHE (2011b) *QAA 'International Students Studying in the UK – guidance for UK
higher education institutions', AMOSSHE, the Student Services Organisation's response*,
www.amosshe.org.uk/sites/default/files/u1567/AMOSSHE%20response%
20to%20%27International%20students%20studying%20in%20the%20UK%20-
%20Guidance%20for%20UK%20higher%20education%20institutions%27%20
consultation%202011%2009%2027.pdf.

AMOSSHE (2011c) *Value and Impact Toolkit*, www.vip.amosshe.org.

AMOSSHE and ARC (2010) *AMOSSHE and ARC Feedback to the SFE Stakeholder Forum*
(internal document).

AUDE (2012) *HESMF*, Association of University Directors of Estates,
www.aude.ac.uk/about/groups.

Bulpitt, G. (ed.) (2012) *Leading the Student Experience: super-convergence of organisation,
structure and business processes*, Series 3, Publication 5, Leadership Foundation for
Higher Education.

Department for Business, Innovation and Skills (2011) *Higher Education: students at the
heart of the system*, Cm 8122,
www.bis.gov.uk/assets/biscore/higher-education/docs/h/11-944-higher-education-
students-at-heart-of-system.pdf.

Hackett, L. (2011) Profile Article: Libby Hackett, *AUA Newslink*, **71**, 4–5.

Heseltine, R., Marsh, S., McKnight, S. and Melling, M. (2009) Super-Convergence:
SCONUL shared-experience meeting, 16 February, *SCONUL Focus*, **46**, 121–4.

Investors in People (2012) IiP Standard, www.investorsinpeople.co.uk.

JM Consulting (2008) *The Sustainability of Learning and Teaching in English Higher
Education*, www.hefce.ac.uk/finance/fundinghe/trac/fssg/FSSGreport.pdf.

Keast, R., Brown, K. A. and Mandell, M. (2007) Getting the Right Mix: unpacking
integration meanings and strategies, *International Public Management Journal*, **10** (1),
9–33.

Melling, M., Selby, E. and Hiles, R. (2011) *Super-Convergence Briefing Note to Professional
Bodies*, unpublished.

NASPA and ACPA (2011) *Consolidation Process Statement*, www.naspa.org/consolidation/.

PARN (2012) *History of PARN*, www.parnglobal.com/history.htm.

QAA (2012) *International Students Studying in the UK: guidance for UK higher education institutions*,
www.qaa.ac.uk/Publications/InformationAndGuidance/Documents/International-students.pdf.

Sargut, G. and Gunther-McGrath, R. (2011) Learning to Live with Complexity, *Harvard Business Review*, September.

Scottish Government (2011) *Putting Learners at the Centre: delivering our ambitions for post-16 education*, APS Group Scotland.

UUK (2011) *Efficiency and Effectiveness in Higher Education*, Universities UK,
www.universitiesuk.ac.uk/Publications/Pages/EfficiencyinHigherEducation.aspx.

West, A. (2011) *Looking Back, Looking Forward, Looking Beyond: AUA 1961–2011*, AUA.

Yip, J., Ernst, C. and Campbell, M. (2011) *Boundary Spanning Leadership*, Center for Creative Leadership.

4

Culture, values and change: observations from three consortia in Canada

Michael Ridley, Canada

Introduction

Cultural change. It's a common phrase these days as most of us grapple with organizational transformation brought about by technological advances, budget constraints and numerous other factors. How do we cause cultural change? What are the new values essential to effective collaborations?

The answers are difficult because the questions are wrong. Anyone trying to 'cause cultural change' or invoke 'new values' has already missed the point. Let's refocus the questions and open up some new opportunities. The more appropriate question is framed as 'how do we nurture effective organizational cultures and their underlying values?'

While discussing culture and values in abstract terms is important, it is often not directly applicable to the real world situations we face in academic libraries. As a result this analysis explores these issues through the lens of specific collaborations and partnerships. The nature and importance of values and culture will be examined by investigating the implementation and sustainability of three Canadian collaborations: the TriUniversity Group of Libraries (TUG), the Scholars Portal of the Ontario Council of University Libraries (OCUL) and the Canadian Research Knowledge Network (CRKN). These three initiatives, while different in scale, approach and focus, share common characteristics which have made them successful. Their longevity (each one is more than ten years old) is evidence of a strong foundation and an ability to adapt.

Background

Collaborations, partnerships, joint ventures and collectives of all sorts and sizes have become commonplace in academic libraries. The USA has been a leader in recognizing the power of working together. The Ohio College Library Center, formed in 1967, gradually transformed into OCLC, the largest library co-operative in the world with over 25,000 member libraries (www.oclc.org). Hirshon's review of OhioLINK (2002), an early and influential state-wide initiative, outlines the organizational and culture adjustments essential to success. This focus continues with the recent creation of innovation projects such as 2CUL, the 'transformative and enduring partnership' of the Cornell University Library and the Columbia University Libraries (www.2cul.org). The extent and depth of collaboration as a key academic library strategy is best illustrated by the formation and growth of the International Coalition of Library Consortia (ICOLC; www.library.yale.edu/consortia), which now has over 200 participating consortia globally.

As the power and effectiveness of working together became apparent, libraries and their staff have had to learn new skills and perspectives. Collaboration is a muscle; the more it is used, the stronger it gets. Conversely, neglect a collaborative initiative and it will atrophy.

It is instructive to note that all three of the collaborations discussed in this chapter arose from adversity: severe budget reductions, dramatic and crippling increases in journal pricing, and the need to respond to rapid technological change are just three of the motivators that led to the formation of these collectives. Although many new partnerships arise in times of challenge, most, as with the three documented here, move well beyond the initial rationale for their inception. This highlights something that many politicians have long known and used to their advantage: never let a good crisis go to waste. The heightened sense of urgency during a time of crisis opens new doors. The unthinkable is now considered, orthodoxies are challenged and sacred cows are on the menu.

Illustrative of this is the percentage of the acquisitions budget spent through consortia. Initially small or negligible (under 5%), now libraries can spend up to 80% of their acquisitions budget through a variety of consortial arrangements. Such dramatic change doesn't happen overnight; it must be carefully nurtured. As collaborations have become essential to the success of academic libraries, change management has become a critical preoccupation for librarians and particularly library directors:

> It is easy to underestimate the difficulty of making the transition to teams and collaboration. During the change of perspective from 'me' to 'us', from 'I' to 'we', and from 'them' to 'us', there are many opportunities to revert to the 'way we always did it.' Sustaining the culture of the collaboration requires vigilance and maintenance.
>
> (Shepherd, Gillham and Ridley, 1999, 336)

Ultimately any collaboration is about mutual self-interest. We work collectively for local and individual benefit. As a result foundational values and organizational cultures exist both in the individual libraries and in the consortium itself. Leslie Weir, University Librarian, University of Ottawa, and former Chair of OCUL and Member of the Board of CRKN, provided some context for Canadian consortia when she wrote:

> In Canada, consortia have been key, and perhaps even more so than in some other countries. We are a relatively homogenous country and yet extremely different at the same time. All of our universities are public, so we do not have the concept of public and private, but our universities are scattered across a very large country. We are bilingual – French and English. We have universities that specialize in various fields (for instance, business and engineering), we have ones that are comprehensive, we have our doctoral-granting institutions, we have our law schools, our medical schools. All this creates both challenges and opportunities.
>
> (Weir, 2008, 582)

As Deb deBruijn, Executive Director of CRKN, notes, many library consortia are key to national or regional agenda for advancing research and higher education (deBruijn, 2004, 10). As such is it critical to think of 'content as infrastructure' and to see academic libraries as essential to public policy initiatives aimed at developing a thriving knowledge-based society.

Before examining the factors and characteristics that impact values and culture in co-operative initiatives, it is useful to have a short overview of each of the consortia that form the basis for these observations.

The TriUniversity Group of Libraries

Founded in 1995, the TriUniversity Group of Libraries (TUG; www.tug-libraries.on.ca) is a partnership of the University of Waterloo, Wilfrid Laurier University and the University of Guelph. The initial agreement called for 'a seamlessly integrated program of library collections and services' (TUG, 1995). Under the auspices of TUG the libraries share a single integrated library system, a discovery layer service, an offsite storage facility, a delivery service that transports requested materials among the libraries on a daily basis, collective resource licensing and purchasing and a data resource service for statistical information. The objectives of the partnership are both pragmatic enhancements to existing services as well as a platform to explore opportunities for new innovations:

> The expansion of access to library resources and the efficiency of access to these resources substantially enrich the processes of scholarship in our universities.

Current fiscal constraint requires that we explore all forms of co-operative activity with a view to achieving efficiencies. (TUG, 2000)

Alongside the service expectations, TUG also articulated some business principles that guide the consortium:

a   Prepare development plans to deliver agreed upon levels of service
b   Have a clear and agreed concept of our core business
c   Optimize human and financial resource investment through sharing common technical and administrative infrastructure, when feasible
d   Ensure, where practical, that the infrastructure facilitates access to public and private sector providers of educational products and services
e   Maintain a healthy balance between collaboration and independence
f   Define models for life cycle investment costs to sustain the infrastructure
g   Develop and maintain appropriate cost-sharing models

(TUG, 2012, para 1).

While much of the initial consortial licensing undertaken by TUG has since moved to regional (OCUL) or national (CRKN) alternatives, TUG continues to provide core services and resources to the three institutions. Much of the recruitment information for students and faculty continues to highlight TUG as a key asset for the individual universities.

Scholars Portal of the Ontario Council of University Libraries

The Ontario Council of University Libraries (OCUL; www.ocul.on.ca) is a consortium of the 21 university libraries in the province. OCUL enhances information services in Ontario and beyond through collective purchasing and shared digital information infrastructure, collaborative planning, advocacy, assessment, research, partnerships, communications and professional development. Under the rubric 'Collaborate, Innovate, Deliver', OCUL has articulated three main objectives:

• collaborate to provide a world-class learning experience for Ontario's students
• expand digital research infrastructure
• provide and preserve academic resources essential for teaching, learning, and research. (OCUL, 2011)

Scholars Portal (http://spotdocs.scholarsportal.info/display/sp/home) provides the technological infrastructure that preserves and provides access to information resources collected and shared by OCUL members. Through the online services of Scholars Portal, students, faculty and researchers have access to millions of e-journal articles, an extensive collection of e-books, an expanding number of social science data sets and an innovative geospatial information system. Scholars Portal also offers an online interlibrary loan platform, an 'Ask a Librarian' e-reference service, support for the RefWorks and WizFolio citation management systems and a variety of other tools designed to aid and enhance academic research in Ontario.

Scholars Portal has become the de facto digital library for each of the members of OCUL. While many of the services and resources are rebranded locally to reflect the local library context, the underlying infrastructure, support and expertise is provided centrally by the Scholars Portal staff at OCUL.

As an affiliate group of the Council of Ontario Universities (COU), the major advocacy group for universities in Ontario, OCUL is well connected to the strategic planning and policy development initiatives of the university presidents and their chief academic officers. This strong linkage between the libraries and the executive heads of the universities has been important in securing external funding and informing the academic leadership of key trends and developments.

The Canadian Research Knowledge Network

The Canadian Research Knowledge Network (CRKN; www.crkn.ca) is a partnership of Canadian universities dedicated to expanding digital content for the academic research enterprise in Canada. Through the co-ordinated leadership of librarians, researchers and administrators CRKN undertakes large-scale content acquisition and licensing initiatives in order to build knowledge infrastructure and research capacity in Canada's universities. CRKN collaborates with 75 university members and provides access to over 900,000 researchers and students. The organization brings together universities in ten provinces, speaking two official languages (French and English) and with diverse degree and programme offerings, and puts in place a national foundation for acquiring scholarly research content in digital formats.

Initiated in 2000 as the Canadian National Site Licensing Project (CNSLP), a federally funded research initiative, CRKN incorporated in 2004 and has since expanded its membership and broadened its licensing programs. The consortium is inclusive. Member universities are committed to licensing a broad portfolio of research content from multiple vendors, with resources acquired available equally to all participants. Using an innovative model licence and a well designed negotiating process and strategy, CRKN has built strong relationships with vendors as it also secured cost-effective deals for its members.

In 2011 CRKN secured nearly $100 million worth of licensing and purchases on behalf of its members. Currently CRKN manages 44 national licences from publishers such as Elsevier, Springer, Wiley-Blackwell, Oxford University Press, Cambridge University Press and the American Chemical Society (CRKN, 2011).

Values: a cautionary note

Management and leadership books consistently identify values as crucial to organizational effectiveness and personal commitment. Widely read texts such as *The Leadership Challenge* (Kouzes and Posner, 2008) and *The Future of Management* (Hamel, 2007) emphasize the pre-eminent role of values (both individual and institutional) in shaping a clear direction and establishing a strong foundation. Articulated values tell our community what is important to us and what they can expect from us. They also guide our choices and decisions about how we operate our organizations. As a result we spend considerable time working on our values. We hold workshops and organize information sessions. We are careful to be inclusive in these gatherings, inviting all staff, representative users and others who are impacted by our resources and services. At the end of all this we clean up the language, post them on our website, and then, sometimes (perhaps quite often), actually live them.

The values so derived are important and useful but they are not actually the values that inform the organization. As much as we would like to think otherwise, values are not documented, they are revealed. The real value-system of any organization is the one illustrated by its actions and its processes. Think of values not as a definitive set of preconditions but rather as an evolving ecology in which, through time and visibility, the actual organization emerges. This is important because it is easy to identify libraries or groups that articulate one set of values (agreed to once upon a time by all staff) but actually live by something completely different.

Contemporary academic libraries must manage interactions with a large number of organizations and their respective value systems. Individual universities and libraries have expressed values but so too do the various consortia that we have come to rely on. As a result, the interdependency of these organizations brings with it a web or matrix of values, lived or stated, that need to be understood and mediated. Values define and motivate individual actions, while culture operationalizes these in an organizational context. This is not to say that values cannot or should not be developed, or that a conflict of values is inevitable in a multi-consortial environment. Rather it suggests that a more organic approach to the understanding and expression of values is necessary.

Characteristics of culture and change in consortia

What do consortial experiences tell us about values, culture and change? TUG, OCUL and CRKN all have long histories during which the actions and attitudes of the members and the organizations reveal characteristics that define how consortia operate and the effect they have on staff and the individual member organizations. The observations in the rest of this chapter provide insights into how future consortia must be structured and operated if they wish to interoperate with their member institutions and enhance their effectiveness as collectives. Nurturing values and effective organizational cultures arise from attention to core elements in any collaboration. The following observations are signals, signposts or opportunities that can assist in decoding the health of consortia and in laying the foundations for healthy cultures and aligned values.

Shared objectives

Common, shared objectives are the obvious core of any collaboration. It is surprising, therefore, that many co-operative ventures lack a clear articulation of exactly what these are. There is a reason for this. Many collaborations, the better ones, are not about solving just a current, acute problem but building capacity and capability for a more ambiguous future. They are tools or vehicles for growth and evolution. Since we don't always know clearly where we are going or exactly how we will get there, these partnerships are leaps of faith. On the surface, while collaborations are tasked with 'buying this' or 'implementing that', the larger and more profound objective is to collectively transform the participating libraries by giving them more capability than they had separately.

Defining shared objectives is critical. However, overly specifying those objectives is a recipe for trouble. This will unnecessarily focus on the here and now, and limit the possibility that the partnership could move into broader and different areas.

Having said all this, finding common ground is essential. TUG arose because each library was considering a new integrated library system, Scholars Portal started because few of the individual OCUL members could implement an effective digital library service on their own and CRKN arose as a result of budget pressures for scholarly journals and the need to move to e-journals. While each continues to have these as core purposes, all have moved into areas that were largely unconsidered during the formative years.

An example of this is the decision of OCUL to extend its digital services to non-OCUL institutions by acting as a service provider. Taking on external clients for financial gain was not part of the initial vision and yet the values that guided the collaborative model among OCUL members also informed the service provider model for paying clients. Monetizing the collaboration was seen as consistent with the original objectives.

Shared objectives evolve and the purpose of any consortium can change over time. In fact a consortium that 'sticks to its knitting' is likely one becoming less and less valuable to its members.

Trust

At the heart of any collaborative venture is trust. Trust is the glue that keeps an initiative together and makes it effective. Without a deliberate attempt to build trust, a partnership will wither. For some people trust is a natural reaction; you immediately have their trust but you can lose it with your actions. For others trust must be earned, typically, through working together.

Pilot projects, working groups, opportunities to exchange ideas, even purely social engagements all create the foundation for trust to emerge or flourish. In the formative days of TUG, staff from all three institutions were brought together to learn together. The focus of the training sessions varied but the real objective was to build confidence in each other. Similarly, TUG launched numerous working groups and task groups, almost certainly more than were really necessary, in order to allow the work assignments to act as foundations for trust.

Don't assume trust is hierarchical or only important to professional staff (i.e. librarians and managers). While it is absolutely true that the library directors must trust each other and visibly demonstrate this to the staff of the libraries, trust accrues in a library in very idiosyncratic ways. Staff in all areas of the library need to be engaged and committed.

Often trust is forged during times of conflict or strain. Difficult situations both challenge trust but also solidify it. As a result nurturing trust is probably a better metaphor than 'winning' or 'building' trust. It relies on leaders who are comfortable with the expertise and instincts of their staff and on staff who are willing to build new relationships across organizational boundaries.

Getting to know each other

Since the University of Waterloo and Wilfrid Laurier University are virtually across the street from each other and the University of Guelph is only 20km away, it was surprising that the staff, especially the librarians, really didn't know each other very well. As observed, since trust is forged by working together, a key priority was to create opportunities for staff to get to know each other.

In addition to the various work assignments, TUG placed a singular emphasis on the social aspects of the consortium. We hosted numerous parties for all staff with special buses to bring folks together. It was all about the food, drink, music, and community. No work, just fun (and the briefest possible requisite speeches by the university librarians!).

The importance of face-to-face interactions during the early phase of the consortium or any new projects of the consortium can't be overestimated. While much of the work of TUG (or any of the other groups) is now conducted via email, shared systems, social media or whatever, the initial 'getting to know you' process is almost always in person.

The challenge is different for consortia that are geographically dispersed. OCUL attempts to address this by hosting a series of 'Scholars Portal Days' designed to bring staff, mostly librarians and managers, together. These events are used to review, plan and simply to provide professional development. The consortium staff work diligently to make these compelling and valuable days. As a result they are now a 'must attend' meeting for many.

In a similar way, CRKN has fashioned its annual meeting, a legal requirement to enact the business of the corporation, into a multi-day conference with workshops, keynote speakers, 'birds of a feather'-type sessions and awards ceremonies. CRKN has hosted a completely online annual meeting and currently offers a hybrid meeting which includes online and face-to-face communication.

In the examples of OCUL and CRKN, it is critical that the libraries are willing to fund the costs for staff to participate. This extra cost of consortial involvement, difficult for some of the smaller institutions, is a concrete demonstration of the importance of face-to-face communication to relationship building.

Loss of control and authority

One clear outcome of consortial purchasing has been the loss of control and authority at the local level regarding collection development. Previously libraries, and specifically collections librarians, built their own collections quite deliberately. Each library had detailed collections development policies, procedures and processes often approved through university governance processes. In some cases individual monographs were hand selected or refused in response to those policies.

Buying or licensing through consortia changed all that. Leveraging the purchasing power of the collective meant relinquishing much local responsibility for individual collection development. Not everyone was happy about this. It took some time for librarians (and directors) to accept the trade-offs involved. The debate about the value of the Big Deal is, in part, predicated on the desire to return to local control over collections. Both Frazier (2005) and Friend (2003) question the cost effectiveness of the Big Deal approach and suggest that large-scale purchases have resulted in collections unresponsive to the specific needs of the local library's users.

Releasing control and authority to a collective can only occur if there is trust in that group and accountability back to the members or those responsible at the local level. Library directors have institutional responsibility for their library. If things go awry, they will be held accountable. The bargain implicit in consortial initiatives is that releasing control and authority at the local level gains other capacities and capabilities that would otherwise be unattainable. Some library directors and libraries are able to accept that situation; others chafe at it throughout the entire process.

The Negotiations Resource Team (NRT) of CRKN is responsible for negotiations with all the vendors. This small team comprises collections of librarians, procurement professionals, IT experts and consortium staff. They establish the list of products to be acquired, set the criteria for negotiations, create requests for proposals (RFPs), draft proposed licences, directly negotiate with vendors and then present the final agreements to members for their acceptance (most CRKN deals are opt-in/opt-out).

The CRKN deals are large and complex, and must address the needs (and the financial capabilities) of a very diverse membership. The negotiations must also be conducted in a fair manner, with complete confidentiality. In the initial period of the development of consortial purchasing it was challenging to keep members, particularly other collections librarians, involved and informed. Often only limited information could be released to the membership during the negotiations process. Similarly, it was difficult, if not impossible, to seek advice from the membership during those negotiations.

As a result tensions emerged when deals were announced. The NRT was viewed as out of touch with members and of working in a closed, even defensive, manner. CRKN responded by creating an online forum, regional meetings and enhanced procedures to involve collections librarians and university librarians earlier in the process. All these initiatives served to engage members while still empowering the NRT to do their work. It was critical for the NRT to have the independence to negotiate on behalf of members. It was equally critical that members had confidence in the NRT.

Differential benefits and cost allocation

Most consortia comprise dissimilar libraries; there are differences in location, size, mandate, philosophy and virtually any other dimension possible. In fact the strength of an effective consortium is often not that the members are alike but that they are different and quite diverse. However, within that diversity, a partnership must find common ground.

OCUL consists of 21 member libraries. The largest, the University of Toronto, has over 60,000 students while the smallest, Algoma University, has less than 1500 students. Both are active participants in virtually all OCUL initiatives. How can both derive value in an equal way? The answer is, they don't. Members derive differential benefits from participation in OCUL; the benefits are not equal but they are equitable. The consortium works diligently to ensure this is the case and that it is well understood by its members.

Scholars Portal is a good example of this. With an annual budget of over $3 million (excluding the cost of the licences and other content), the system was designed to be located and operated primarily by the University of Toronto. Many of the decisions about the evolution of Scholars Portal are influenced by the directions preferred by Toronto. This is not a surrender to the whims of the larger institution but part of the structure and strategy that creates value for the largest members as well as the smallest.

Scholars Portal is highly valuable to both Toronto and Algoma albeit it in very different ways. Toronto easily has the resources to implement and sustain a service like Scholars Portal by itself. However, in collaborating through OCUL it benefits from the substantial contributions of others (the University of Toronto pays approximately $0.25 for every $1 of value gained through OCUL).

The point about equity and differential benefits is that it mitigates tension around cost allocation formulae that often don't include all the potential factors (particularly the benefits side of the equation). For example, TUG struggled for a number of years to distribute costs effectively across the three institutions. Finally the university librarians engaged a third party (Ernst & Young, a consulting firm) to recommend a solution (Ernst & Young, 2000).The consultants worked with the university librarians to help them understand the nature of metrics and to focus on key metrics as surrogates for value and cost. This intervention resolved many underlying tensions (among the university librarians as well as the staff of the libraries). The resulting metrics have now been in place for over ten years.

A more difficult struggle occurred in CRKN. The diversity was greater in part because the consortium was larger, consisting of 75 members spread across the country with regional and even linguistic differences. Creating cost allocation formulae for CRKN became an obsession. There were serious conflicts over costs to individual members for particular licences. Fairness, equity and perceived value are difficult to align across a large membership. For the most part a disproportionate amount of the costs resided with the five largest institutional members. While members usually have the option of opting out of CRKN deals, it is also true that without the largest institutions, the negotiating power of CRKN would be diminished (with resulting financial increases to other members). CRKN has moved increasingly to alternative methods to allocate costs and align them more with institutional value. However, it remains an ongoing discussion. It is perhaps illustrative of the capacity of CRKN to engage openly with these concerns that the large institutions remain members and new universities have joined.

The art of the possible

Because collaborations are successful and beneficial there is a natural desire to do more, expand the reach, or explore new options. This can be very good but it can also be problematic. While collaborations built on solid, strategic foundations are able to grow into new areas, those that have a more limited vision of their purpose can resist such changes. The founding library directors of TUG often referred to it as the 'art of the possible'. The programmes of TUG were those that were achievable (possible), not those that seemed beneficial.

For example, given the geographic proximity of the three libraries one would think that significant collection rationalization (and relocation) would be an obvious opportunity. Since there was a shared catalogue with an effective delivery system among the libraries, why not reduce duplication, expand unique purchases and specialize collections and expertise? At a strategic level, this is perfectly obvious and advantageous. On a more pragmatic level, it was a non-starter. While librarians saw this as a useful direction, faculty were outraged. Despite the fact that it would increase the resources available to them in their specific disciplines, the idea that the urban geography books and journals (to pick an example) would be at a campus other than theirs was anathema. The art of the possible was recognizing, before going too far, that such a perfectly reasonable direction was not going to work.

Appealing to the 'art of the possible' can sometimes be used as a defence against change. Arguing 'it can't be done' or 'we tried this before and it didn't work' are common ways this defence is used. However, more often it is a clear realization of the limits of any collaboration and the fact that pushing an initiative beyond that limit could have negative and long lasting consequences to the partnership as a whole.

Broadening the community of practice

A tremendous benefit of consortia is the ability to build capacity and capability through sharing and joint actions. All academic libraries constitute a community of practice. This perspective on our professional roles enriches how we approach our work and especially how we develop ourselves as librarians. Co-operative ventures broaden this community of practice by engaging professional staff across institutional boundaries. We learn from each other, we challenge each other and we build new mental models of what our roles are and how we perform them.

Critically this is an active, goal oriented engagement. It is not like communing at a conference or workshop. It is work focused, deadline based, resource constrained and ultimately very creative. As such it is real work and the resulting learning has a deep and profound impact on professional growth.

In TUG, a particularly important resource was the ongoing involvement of what was then the Office of Management and Leadership Services (OMLS) of the Association of Research Libraries (ARL). OMLS staff led various workshops and sessions for TUG professional staff focused on management practices and team building. Working with OMLS allowed the libraries to study and practice the same philosophy of library management and administration. This foundation curriculum was important in aligning the expectations, procedures and attitudes of staff as TUG evolved. The values driving the decision-making of the consortium were discussed, explored and confirmed during those sessions.

Local issues and consortial impact

Consortia are tools for leveraging common purpose but all consortia ultimately comprise individual institutional members. The organizational health and vitality of the consortia are always impacted by whatever is happening in the individual institutions. Typically those local issues are different for each institution at different times. One library may be experiencing budget reductions while another has just received a substantial increase. As a result one wants to reduce consortium costs while the other is ready to invest in new projects.

One response from the consortium is to ignore this and say such issues can't be accommodated because they are beyond its control. This is a poor idea. While it is true that consortia don't manage the member institutions, they are impacted by what is happening in each member library. Consortia must have very effective ears and eyes among their members. Knowing how each is evolving, struggling or thriving is essential to leading the collective to common solutions.

An important outcome of this is to see a consortium as a normal, definitive part of the local organization. For the University of Guelph, TUG is not 'it' but 'us'. Scholars Portal is Guelph's digital library and the staff of Scholars Portal are effectively Guelph staff. It would be a clear indication of this if the consortium staff appeared on all our organization charts, but despite our commitment to and reliance on consortia, there often remains a demarcation between the 'real' staff of the library and consortial staff. The latter are viewed less central to the organization.

This is especially important as budget challenges at the local level almost always result first in trying to reduce consortial expenditures. The remote or distant nature of a consortium means that many find it is easier to cut them first. However, from a budget or service perspective, consortia are almost always financially attractive and cost effective. A modest investment typically reaps much larger rewards. Hence reducing local costs first is actually a better strategy.

Of course (to give an extreme example), laying off local staff while increasing consortial staff during times of budget constraint may be so politically untenable that individual libraries are required to make suboptimal financial decisions. Bridging the distance between the member institution and the consortium is important. Consortial staff and local staff must be seen to be on the same team, wanting the same outcomes and experiencing the same constraints or opportunities.

Governance

As collaborations have matured, so has our attitude towards governance. Leading a small partnership required aligned leaders. A large-scale collaboration requires formal governance. When a collaboration grows to have its own staff, the nature of the engagement and involvement of the member libraries (and their leaders) changes irrevocably. In small collaborations the library directors, for example, can collectively make the management decisions. The 'board' is often the entire complement of directors. Moving a collaboration into a more formal organization requires a different level of engagement. For example, CRKN is incorporated separately and OCUL is part of a larger non-profit organization, while TUG remains an agreement among the institutions. Not all library directors, library staff or university administrators are able make this transition.

With an executive director (and their staff) comes a board of directors and a community of members. Each of these has very different responsibilities and obligations. Members don't determine policy, the board doesn't manage staff and the executive director doesn't run the libraries. Understanding the different roles and letting each perform their designated responsibilities is crucial. Many partnerships experience deep conflict because individuals exceed or ignore their accountability.

The most common challenges stem from board members who want to run the organization and direct the staff, or an executive director who wants to 'guide' ('manipulate') the decisions of the board. With the current multitude of overlapping organizations, collaborations and partnerships it has never been more important to ensure effective board orientation. Knowing what the board is accountable for and what its job is remains critical. Frankly, this is done far less than is necessary. Guides to board member duties and responsibilities (Kelly and Frederick, 1999) and to effective orientation processes (Ingram, 2003) are essential resources for any formally governed consortium.

While part of any board orientation is a clear understanding of responsibilities and accountabilities (including specific legal and fiduciary obligations, which are binding and serious), another key purpose is to build community among the board members. This is done not to forge a happy, complacent family but rather to ensure that a comfortable level of interaction exists so that difficult and contentious issues can be raised.

CRKN undertook a substantial organizational review arising from a lack of clarity around board roles. Tension between the Board members and some institutional members over decision-making and accountability reflected a misunderstanding of the role a board plays in a membership organization. Some members, who were previously in a position to exert individual direction on the organization, found the Board a limit on their personal influence. They were unwilling to accept the responsibility delegated to the Board. The loss of control discussed earlier with respect to collections librarians applies to university librarians as well. The context is different but the tension and dislocation are the same.

Managing transparency and conflict

Collaborations, like marriages, have their moments of conflict and doubt. This is especially true of initiatives that have long histories and have evolved over that period. Members can lose their way and lose their resolve. As a result, concerns about directions, costs, expertise, succession or leadership can creep in. If these issues can be raised and addressed through a clear governance model and process, most organizations are able to address these issues successfully, even if this means drastic actions such as terminating an executive director's contract, refocusing the organization or even winding down the organization. However, the lack of a transparent process can be disastrous.

The rise of activist members of corporate boards in recent years is in many ways a reaction to complacency and lack of purpose on the part of those boards. In Canada, the power struggle for Board control at the iconic Canadian Pacific Railway is illustrative of how contentious this can get (McNish, Jang and Silcoft, 2012). While activism is most common in the corporate environment, there is evidence that this is also occurring in higher education, affecting boards with a direct relation to academic libraries (Bastedo, 2005; Immerwahr, 2011). The activist board member is often reflecting similar concerns among the stakeholders.

It would be a cliché to note that effective, ongoing communication is central to avoiding conflict or addressing it when it arrives. Many organizations have learned to do this very well. Creating multiple communications channels that engage directors, library staff, external partners (vendors) and even library users in different ways using different tools is a key strategy for transparency. CRKN, for example, has created forums and communication vehicles that correspond specifically to different groups within the member organizations. Hence general e-newsletters are matched by an online licence information exchange for collections librarians, personal e-updates from the Executive Director for library directors and OpenLine, a series of teleconferences or webinars with guest presenters on timely topics relevant to library staff, vendors and researchers.

Conclusion

At the outset we asked 'how do we nurture effective organizational cultures and their underlying values?' The observations from the TUG, Scholars Portal of the OCUL and the CRKN illustrate both prerequisites and warnings. All suggest that effective organizational cultures and aligned values arise not from strategic plans, executive decrees, or merely wishful thinking, but from a consistent focus on how individuals interact within an organizational setting.

The continuous transformation of academic libraries as they engage in increasingly broad and complex collaborative initiatives means that long-held values will be challenged, traditional practices will be abandoned, and organizations will be reshaped to suit new purposes. As a result it will require leaders at all levels and in all places of the organization to adopt strategies and techniques that bring to the surface key concerns and enable new ways of working together.

Values are revealed and culture is nurtured. Successful organizations understand these dynamics and facilitate processes that engender healthy workplaces and effective institutions.

References

Bastedo, M. (2005) The Making of an Activist Governing Board, *The Review of Higher Education*, **28** (4), 551-70.

Canadian Research Knowledge Network (CRKN) (2011) *Annual Report 2010-2011*, www.crkn.ca/sites/default/files/annualReports/en/CRKN_AR_EN_Print_2010-11.pdf.

deBruijn, D. (2004) *Consortia Collaboration: the view from Canada*, presentation given at the International Coalition of Library Consortia, Fall 2004, 28 October, Barcelona, http://eprints.rclis.org/handle/10760/5821/1.

Ernst & Young (2000) *Tri-University Group of Libraries: cost sharing project*, www.staff.tug-libraries.on.ca/documents/tuccostsharing.html.

Frazier, K. (2005) What's the Big Deal? *The Serials Librarian*, **48** (1-2), 49-59.

Friend, F. (2003) Big Deal - Good Deal? Or Is There a Better Deal?, *Learned Publishing*, **16** (2), 153-5.

Hamel, G. (2007) *The Future of Management*, Harvard Business School Press.

Hirshon, A. (2002) Library Strategic Alliances and the Digital Library in the 1990s: the OhioLINK experience, *The Journal of Academic Librarianship*, **21** (5), 383-6.

Immerwahr, J. (2011) Still on the Sidelines: what role will trustees play in higher education reform?, *Public Agenda*, www.publicagenda.org/files/pdf/STILLONTHESIDELINES.pdf.

Ingram, R. (2003) *New Trustee Orientation: a guide for public colleges and universities*, Association of Governing Boards of Universities and Colleges.

Kelly, H. and Frederick, M. (1999) *Duties and Responsibilities of Directors of Non-Profit Corporations*, Canadian Society of Association Executives.

Kouzes, J. and Posner, B. (2008) *The Leadership Challenge*, 4th edn, Jossey-Bass.

McNish, J., Jang, B. and Silcoff, S. (2012) The Story behind the All-out War to Control CP, *The Globe and Mail*, 14 January, www.theglobemail.com/globe-investor/the-story-behind-the-all-out-war-to-control-cp/article1358769/?page=all.

Ontario Council of University Libraries (OCUL) (2011) *Strategic Plan 2011*, www.ocul.on.ca/node/29.

Shepherd, M., Gillham, V. and Ridley, M. (1999) The Truth Is in the Details: lessons in inter-university collaboration, *Library Management*, **20** (6), 332-7.

TriUniversity Group of Libraries (TUG) (1995) *Integrated Programme Development: a tri-lateral statement of intent for the libraries of the University of Guelph, the University of Waterloo, and Wilfrid Laurier University*, www.lib.uwaterloo.ca/News/UWLibDocs/joint_agree.html.

TriUniversity Group of Libraries (TUG) (2000) The First Five Years: a report from the TriUniversity Group of Libraries, http://staff.tug-libraries.on.ca/documents/firstfive2.html.

TriUniversity Group of Libraries (TUG) (2012) *Business Principles*, www.tug-libraries.on.ca/tugprin.

Weir, L. (2008) A Conversation with Leslie Weir, *The Serials Librarian*, **55** (4), 577-97.

5 Managing complex change collaboratively

Margaret Weaver, University of Cumbria, UK

Acknowledgements

The author would like to thank other members of the Change Academy Team, Julie Berry, Grace Hudson, Liz Jolly, Alison Mackenzie, Maxine Melling, Jo Norry, Liz Waller and Sue White, for their creative contributions to the contents of the chapter.

Introduction

The Higher Education Academy (HEA) and the Leadership Foundation for Higher Education (LFHE) supports UK higher education institutions (HEIs) in achieving complex cultural change through their annual Change Academy (CA) programme. This chapter describes the creation of a new collaborative network of academic libraries in the north of England following an intensive cross-institutional planning initiative and presence at the HEA CA Conference and subsequent work in 2010-11, which launched the COLLABORATE! project and the Northern Collaboration (NC). The process enabled the vision of key individuals to be converted into a tangible entity. The interplay between creative thinking, conceptual activity, teamwork and action is thought to be a constructive way to bring about complex change. I describe the thinking behind the approach, and how this was achieved at a time of volatility (and opportunity) in higher education (HE).

Context
Drivers for change in higher education

The key drivers for radical and fundamental change in the UK HE and HE library sector have been well rehearsed by many recently (Nicholas et al., 2010; Harper and Corrall, 2011; Kidd, 2010). These changes are underpinned by a raft of UK government reforms arising from a constraining financial climate and the perceived need for additional accountability in the HE system; this is coupled with the desire to give more power to the recipients of HE, most particularly students and employers.

Notable government proposals now being implemented are contained in the White Paper on HE reforms (Department for Business, Innovation and Skills, 2011), the UK Independent Review into Higher Education Funding and Student Finance, the Browne Report (Department for Business, Innovation and Skills, 2010), and the UK Government Comprehensive Spending Review 2010, which forecast a 40% reduction in core funding to the HE sector for taught provision, a sum of £2.9 billion by 2014–15 (HM Treasury, 2010). In addition a complex system of student-number controls exists aiming to increase flexibility across the HE market (for example HE delivered by commercial organizations). Consequently institutions have less certainty than previously about their recruitment outcomes and income levels. At the same time research intensive universities are facing changes to the research funding regime in the UK and will have to make significant efficiency savings as a result of the Wakeham Review (RCUK, 2011). Research Councils UK (RCUK) summarizes the situation:

> Collectively across the entire research community – in HEIs, institutes as well as research and funding councils – it must be demonstrated that savings have been achieved in order to achieve greater efficiency for the investment of public money. All of the funds saved will remain within the ring fence to be reinvested in science and research.
> (RCUK, 2011)

In Europe, similar ambitious reforms are on the way, including the Horizon 2020 initiative to 'establish a single strategic framework for Research and Innovation' across Europe (European Commission, 2011).

This calls into question the nature of HE in the UK, where key political messages are that universities must become more effective, offer better value for money and understand their cost base more, while maintaining their world reputation for excellence (Universities UK, 2011). Set against the development of significant new mechanisms, such as student charters (Student Charter Group, 2011) and student feedback systems, a revised Quality Code for Higher Education (QAA, 2012), the removal of the tuition fee cap for universities and HE colleges and the introduction of student finance reform (including the provision of loans to part-time students) advocated by Browne (Department for Business, Innovation and Skills, 2010), the HE landscape looks entirely different in 2012 than it did in 2009 (for an overview of the many changes see Business, Innovation and Skills Committee, 2011).

In parallel with these developments is the expectation that HEIs will work together more effectively in a competitive environment (and many are), where shared services (also known as above-campus services) will exist on a much larger scale than previously. The UK government is thus encouraging innovation in shared services design, further enabled by proposals to remove the Value Added Tax (VAT) payable on shared services by charitable institutions, as set out in the draft Finance Bill 2012 (HEFCE, n.d.). Against this complex backdrop, the challenges present within an academic library setting are doubly significant and are outlined below.

Challenges for academic libraries

1 *A changing student profile:* Given increased tuition fees and the fact students are paying full fees to their institution as opposed to HEIs being funded directly by central government, there is an increased diversity in the range of service requirements in the student offer, which means heightened expectations with potentially less resource.

2 *The curriculum:* There is an increase in types of course and range of delivery methods, such as active learning and distance learning, new subjects, work-based learning, internationalization of the curriculum and a renewed emphasis on employability across all programmes, which means a variety of learning styles must be accommodated.

3 *Organizational structures:* The growing trend for convergence and super-convergence of academic learning support and library services means service delivery via multi-professional teams is becoming more commonplace (Bulpitt, 2012; also referenced in Chapters 6 and 9 in this volume).

4 *Professional skills and knowledge:* New roles are emerging for supporters of learning, including library staff (for example new and emerging learner-support roles across the student experience), leading to different staff dispositions and skills that are needed in the new learning environment.

5 *Uncertainty:* Financial and political constraints and the changes to government policies, and the volatility of the HE market, including the escalating costs of learning content, mean that successful ways of managing in the past are no guide to managing in the future (see particularly Chapter 1).

6 *Performance measurement:* There is an increasing requirement for libraries to demonstrate sustainability, value and impact at an organizational and national level, for example the renewed emphasis in the UK on research, intellectual property assets and knowledge transfer, to deliver UK economic advantage.

7 *Technology and social media:* The imperative to harness emergent and fast-

moving technologies to design innovative services that enthuse, engage and retain students has never been more important (a key feature of Chapter 7).

8   *Shared services:* A renewed emphasis on developing shared services, as an effective way to deliver services in these challenging economic times, whether that is for goods or for services, is under way (Davies, 2011).

Given the above factors, it follows that HEIs and their libraries are facing unprecedented change, placing a complex set of demands on strategic library managers. The financial and political imperatives to work beyond one's own institution have become of central concern and occupy much of the thinking in universities and colleges and indeed across the public sector. Writing in 2010, Jubb successfully summed up the key challenges facing academic libraries in difficult economic times, concluding:

> If they [academic libraries] are to develop new services or enhance existing ones . . ., libraries must tackle three key challenges:
>
> • First, they must reduce if not eliminate what is routine in order to make space for new activities, for it is unlikely that additional resources or funding will be available. Outsourcing of what can be done more efficiently or effectively by others is likely to be part of the answer in areas including cataloguing and the hosting of library websites.
> • Second, they must ensure that users are fully engaged in the development and implementation of new services.
> • Third, they must develop new models of working co-operatively to exploit the resources and expertise of their colleagues in the sector as a whole. A recent project sponsored by SCONUL to develop a business case for shared services for all UK university libraries is a significant example of work of this kind.
>
> (Jubb, 2010, 144)

(For details of recent shared services projects pertaining to academic libraries see reports by the Joint Information Systems Committee (JISC) and SCONUL (the Society of College, National and University Libraries), n.d.; Higher Education Library Technology Group, n.d.)

In order to exploit the opportunities and mitigate the risks inherent in this new HE context, a group of 27 academic libraries in the north of England (see section on the NC below) agreed to attempt to influence the impact of the new and constrained economic operating environment by identifying options for further co-operation. It was felt that by sharing experience and joint ventures, new models of service delivery could emerge. The Collaboration concluded that complex cultural change such as was envisaged would not be easily achieved as part of 'the day job', and a project bid to the HEA CA programme would create the time and space to develop realistic and tangible plans: the COLLABORATE! project. The CA team would work together over a period of 18 months concerning themselves with fundamental questions, such as what can be achieved by collaborative working juxtaposed with the requirement to remain competitive. I call this dilemma the *collaboration paradox*.

The collaboration paradox

As demonstrated in the first part of this chapter, the UK government and the Higher Education Funding Council for England (HEFCE) are clear that universities and colleges must change; they must work closely together to enhance the student experience and be more effective businesses. Academic libraries face similar challenges to their parent institution as they seek to position themselves positively in the market and in supporting their institutional strategic aims. There has been much discussion about possible future scenarios for academic libraries (Curtis, 2011) but there is still uncertainty about whether the future landscape will include the need to collaborate very actively or whether a very competitive landscape will reduce the appetite for collaboration.

The changing conditions mean that organizations on the one hand can no longer afford to work in isolation from each other as they seek to maximize efficiency and control costs (developing shared services, for example), and on the other hand are becoming more competitive because of UK government student-number controls, for example. Potentially, then, HEIs and their libraries are becoming less willing to share, in order to maintain their market position, which would seem to fly in the face of working co-operatively (however, see Chapter 6 on leadership). All this is happening at a time when HEIs are working very hard to involve and meet the demands of their increasingly vocal customer base.

The collaboration paradox was therefore one of the central tensions that concerned the CA team seeking to develop new models of service delivery among a diverse set of HEIs and was also the reason why the COLLABORATE! project (to set up a new collaboration in the north of England) was accepted by the HEA on to the year-long CA programme in 2010-11.

Library collaborations in the north of England

To further set the scene I will next outline the academic library collaboration landscape in the north of England.

North West Academic Libraries (NoWAL) was formed in the 1990s from the Consortium of Academic Libraries in Manchester (CALIM) (Blunden-Ellis, 1994), a metropolitan network of HEIs delivering reciprocal access services and staff development, and seeking procurement advantage in a single conurbation (Manchester) with a philosophy of 'enlightened self-interest'.

In early 2000, membership was widened to include HE colleges, in recognition of the importance of the north-west region and of the UK government's regionalism agenda. Similarly in the north-east of England other collaborations were/are active, for example North East and Yorkshire Academic Libraries (NEYAL) and White Rose University Consortium, all indicating the wealth of library collections, expertise and services which deserved to be recognized in 'the north'. NoWAL had particular success and a strong reputation in collaboration and delivering projects, joint procurement, conferences, a high quality staff-development programme and networking events over a significant period of time. The NC project was keen to build on this expertise.

Indeed the success and confidence of NoWAL and other consortia led to the premise that working in concert across all mission groups in the north of England, in a coherent way, had potential advantage. Hence in October 2009, following an informal meeting of interested parties, a commitment was made by over 20 university librarians in the north of England to meet regularly over a period of two years to see if there were opportunities for further collaborative practice building on the successful partnerships already in place; the NC was conceived.

The Northern Collaboration

The NC consists of 27 academic libraries in the north of England. As mentioned earlier, the view of the group was that joining together to plan the future would lead to even more divergent thinking and new services delivered differently. By generating alternative types of clusters and co-operations, strategic benefit for minimum outlay could be achieved. There was also a recognition by members that the changing context of HE needs different approaches, to assure value for money and to align space, learning resources and support with an ever-decreasing unit of resource.

Consequently there was an appetite to harness the collective purpose of all the partners and develop future services in a more imaginative way. 'The North' was felt to be a sensible grouping and a manageable number of institutions that collectively could work together to good effect. In summary, the vision is to change the way that academic libraries and learning support services conceive their strategic direction using collaboration as a way to challenge and transform services and find new ways of working.

This early intent was an important commitment positioning the group to maximize their impact on learning, teaching and research and to devise new methods of engaging beyond well established approaches to library collaboration (good as these are). At one of the early meetings of the NC it became clear that the new and constrained economic operating environment offered both challenges and opportunities for academic libraries and their staff, which could be exploited more effectively by sharing of experience and joint ventures and by alignment of our strategies to the increased market forces of HE. As mentioned earlier, the COLLABORATE! project was conceived as a way to move this complex agenda forward and a bid to the CA was made to assist with the transition.

The Change Academy: COLLABORATE! project

The CA is an annual programme for change managers run by the HEA and the LFHE, both UK publicly funded bodies. The HEA promotes HE by providing strategic advice and co-ordination for the sector, government and funding bodies and others on policies and practices that will impact on and enhance the student experience; it aims to facilitate the professional development and increase the professional standing of staff in HE. The LFHE has been set up to serve the diverse leadership development needs of senior managers in UK universities and colleges, sharing and championing good practice in leadership, governance and management.

The proposal to the CA aimed to address directly the sector's strategic priority of enhancement of the student experience, which has been identified as key to their own strategies by all participating institutions, and meet the challenging financial imperative. At the same time the development of transformational services models, which are founded in collaborative approaches, were central to the philosophy and working practice of the CA team, which consisted of nine of the UK NC institutions:

- the University of Bradford
- the University of Cumbria (lead partner)
- Edge Hill University
- the University of Huddersfield
- Leeds Metropolitan University
- Liverpool John Moores University
- the University of Salford
- Teesside University
- the University of York.

It was important to have the flexibility to develop plans and to be able to engage the other NC partners. Therefore the deliverables in the action plans were themselves subject to change and personalization by the partners, who it was envisaged would opt in or opt out as needed. The CA team also wanted to capture the way of working required in the increased competitive environment and involve additional stakeholders in partners' operating spheres, especially students and senior university decision-makers. The COLLABORATE! project goals were as follows:

1. Identify a range of Federated Library Services whereby a service element or resource might be provided via a partnership to achieve economies of scale:
    - What would these shared services look like?
    - How could they bring about more cost effective and efficient services using a sustainable model by working together?
2. Assess the implications for leadership and identify new staff roles:
    - What will the library job of the future be like if collaboration and partnership are the core objectives?
    - What might this mean for professional frameworks, accreditation, structures and workforce planning and patterns?
3. Feed project outcomes into planning, service reviews, budgeting and evaluation:
    - How to benchmark and assess collaborative initiatives and shared services?
    - How to demonstrate added value and sustainability whilst also enhancing the student experience?
4. Develop a collaborative framework to take advantage of the diversity in the north:
    - How to develop services which take account of the digital domain for example image libraries on a regional scale, cross domain solutions using web 2.0?
    - How to use existing innovations, for example work done in a collaborative context using emergent technologies such as the pilot work done in 2008 on shared services Library Management Systems?

(Adamson et al., 2008)

It was against this backdrop that the team (see above) from the NC took part in the year-long CA in 2010-11, after the COLLABORATE! bid to the HEA was successful.

The Change Academy experience

The CA (www.heacademy.ac.uk/resources/detail/change/change_academy) is now in its tenth year and is a supportive yet challenging framework provided for HEIs to help them create and achieve their change plans. Successful applicants attend the three-day CA conference where experts, tools and techniques are combined with creative thinking tasks that allow change teams to work on their projects and produce an action plan to take back to their own organizations. Most HEIs attending the CA are single institutions; however, our collaboration project consisted of potentially 27 institutions and was therefore seen as innovative, difficult and worthwhile.

The CA process enables creativity by providing teams with the tools, techniques and encouragement for 'co-creation', an idea first developed in the USA (Pittilo, 2005). For example, teams are asked each to prepare for their CA conference by thinking about their conceptions of change and by producing a rich picture of their project that they can share with other teams. A rich picture shows the relationships between parts of the project, the influence of project stakeholders, their connections and motivations for engaging with the project, and environmental detail that will set the forward direction of the desired change. By using a variety of mechanisms, for example text, drawings, photographs, video, speech bubbles and metaphors, the team was able to generate new thinking in an entertaining way (see Monk and Howard, 1998, for a full description of the method). Through this process the team arrived at a consensus about change, acknowledging:

- the many overlaps between the personal and the organizational and the importance of understanding the motivators for personal change, including the value of personal challenge
- that doing things differently (and doing different things) means knowing what to stop as well as what to start
- the importance of having a different mindset, 'letting go', which will lead to a changed state of mind
- that individuals all have differing responses, depending on their outlook; change for some means having fun, being progressive and is developmental and exciting, but for others means threat and uncertainty
- that professional values help with transition, for example the motivation to make a difference and improve services in turn helps librarians to deal with change
- that collaborative partnerships offer new markets and new opportunities, which should be harnessed, especially where current systems and behaviours are not necessarily working.

A shared view was reached on the importance of having goals whether long term or short term, and arising out of the CA process it was agreed that tangible outcomes needed to be defined along with some 'quick wins'.

During the three days of the conference, the team developed the NC 'story', using a variety of techniques (including the rich picture) encouraged by an expert group of facilitators. The power of generating unlikely questions using word association exercises led to different angles and assumptions. For example, thinking about the financial constraints facing library managers, the statement 'senior management need to fund the Library £xxxx', was rephrased using a positive opposite approach: 'we can succeed without £xxx'. This freed up thinking and allowed new, more positive ideas to flourish. Giving and receiving feedback was a core part of the CA and one of the activities – the Liquid Café (Seel, 2006) – was an opportunity for each team to circulate their plans round a series of themed tables, and for others to ask questions and record observations which the team could then acknowledge. The team also undertook a social network analysis to ensure that the right audience for the project was engaged at the right time.

The value of the tasks was to get insights into assumptions on change, to work towards a common understanding, to feed into thinking about change categories and construct possible quick wins, to begin the dialogue about the project in a safe environment and to team-build. At this stage the team focused on how to engage others in the project and changes, given NC institutions are very diverse. Milestones, business models and possible shared service areas were examined to inform the action plan and to inject some realism into the project. By the second day a framework had been developed for the project that could be tested with the CA audience and experts. The team was realistic about whether collaboration would deliver, the need for costing and benchmarking data to build the evidence base for any new service model, and the need for student engagement at a high level to deliver process review and sound future investment. It was agreed that adding value through the project would involve a critical review of current services.

This intensive experience developed individuals' leadership capacity and teamworking abilities as well as generating the actions needed. A strong concept within which to work as a viable collaboration was created including a possible governance structure. The project received endorsement of approach from the LFHE and the HEA facilitator, which all groups are assigned as a critical friend. The team also received tips about how to communicate the change proposals and how to involve senior staff and other stakeholders appropriately, which was invaluable. Expressing the concept of new library clusters in a clear way that each NC partner could potentially benefit from, without being prescriptive, was a major turning point, which would not have been achieved without participation in the CA process.

Change Academy outcomes

It was proposed that the concept and framework for operationalizing the NC could be adopted by all the universities in the north of England, with the ability to opt into the particular services relevant to their own institutions. The proposal was discussed with the wider NC group in October 2010 and it received broad endorsement to move ahead. Those present all agreed that the primary objective should be a cost-benefit one: to save money, time and/or effort or do more with the same or less, and that robust business models underpinning shared services would need to be developed.

In July 2011, the Principles of the NC were defined and a governance structure put into place that included an overarching Steering Group, hosting Director Forums twice a year. Central to the modus operandi is the desire not to create a large administrative overhead, and so far no subscription has been put into place. The commitment of members to the NC over time has yet to be proven, but early signs are favourable and the NC as an entity has emerged with a strong desire to work in three project areas, which are next described.

Northern Collaboration: current initiatives

The COLLABORATE! project developed options for the NC to take forward so that the strategic purpose of the collaboration could be achieved. An extensive list of possible initiatives for the NC was generated by the CA team during and following the CA Conference. These were scrutinized by the project team using the following criteria:

- the cost savings potential
- the shared services potential
- whether the idea provided an element of competitive advantage for institutions
- the level of attractiveness to a wide range of universities and their clients
- the scaleability across institutions and sectors
- the level of duplication (is it already done better by others?)
- the extent to which the idea raised the profile and value of libraries.

As a result three projects are being actively explored, taking a business-centred approach. These are described below:

Project strand 1: infrastructure

The project is to create a presence for the NC which will include a central website bringing together a range of services under the NC banner. This initiative will bring the benefit of making more effective use of publicly funded collections, but will not save money in itself. It will need a critical mass of institutions to participate. It will probably not be viable as an initiative in its own right but only alongside another shared service. There may be issues for some universities that would feel a need to differentiate their services in the new fees world, so brand identity of the NC is being be carefully considered. A longer-term aim under this strand is to widen access to our libraries for all students of the north and work has commenced with interested partners.

Project strand 2: virtual enquiry services

The project is defining and developing a model for library virtual enquiry services which can be shared across the NC. Virtual enquiry services are defined as enquiry services offered via telephone, email or the web, particularly outside core hours of operation when students and staff do not necessarily have ready access to library staff.

It was recognized that each institution will have different needs from the 'service' depending on their aims and current service shape, for example some are converged IT and library services, others not. Currently three scenarios are envisaged around which a virtual service might be developed:

- Model 1: Outsourced service, hosted by external independent organization.
- Model 2: As Model 1 but hosted by member(s) of the NC.
- Model 3: Shared service with contributions from various institutions in the NC.

Core work has begun with mapping current enquiry services across the partners, developing a service specification, designing referral mechanisms, gathering statistics, and benchmarking information on volume and enquiry types, including costings. There will be an emphasis on building a service using Web 2.0 tools.

Project strand 3: technical services and procurement

Various elements of technical services are being explored, including:

- procurement, including e-services as area of greatest potential cost savings, for example patron-driven approaches, but without duplicating at national level

- the sharing of technical processing of books, cataloguing, classification and physical processing
- shared storage possibilities
- integration or strategic joining up of repositories
- shared electronic resource management (for example how partners might engage with the new SCONUL service, mentioned earlier)
- scoping of 'flying' specialists, e.g. archivist, or for catalogue or web interface expertise needed for short intense projects or to build capacity in institutions.

One benefit of conducting the chosen work strands within a regional as opposed to a national setting is the opportunity for tailored approaches to be taken, that are able to draw on national initiatives and apply them at a more local level. Success measures, timescales and risks are also being plotted for each area, which is possibly more realistic on a regional scale.

Implications for library leaders: leading collaboratively

Leading the CA on such a complex project on behalf of many prestigious HE libraries was exciting and daunting at the same time (see also Chapter 6 on leadership). There was a positive outcome and there were few areas that weren't anticipated. However, this was made possible because of the range of mission groups in the make-up of the project team, which meant the diverse views could be taken into account.

The process provided different perspectives on leadership with the creation of a new 'professional community' that transcends structures in one's own institution or immediate sphere of control, as advocated in Chapters 1, 6 and 8. Turn-taking and facilitation of discussions were key requirements of members to ensure joint working where accountabilities are not managerial; inspiring honesty and integrity between team members has been essential to build trust. Personal influence has developed through sharing insights and professional views with team members combined with active listening and being open to new ideas.

From the outset a set of 'rules of engagement for the CA team' were identified: there was agreement to:

- respect the confidentiality of team members and to encourage openness
- be honest (to oneself and to others)
- identify actions at the end of each meeting, and to share tasks and workload
- provide summaries of progress at each meeting
- rotate chairing of project meetings so all team members are equal

- communicate outcomes and process to the NC and home institutions via a communication protocol and strategy
- acknowledge that disagreements may occur but that these will not jeopardize working relationships
- commit to the CA project until complete in 2011–12.

Working with such a diverse group of library directors meant there were varying institutional priorities to consider and team members had continuously to anticipate the impact of their ideas on the wider NC members. Involving stakeholders and managing communications effectively were all part of the work process and significant time was committed to these areas. Selling the idea at one's home institution had to be carefully thought through and seemed harder once we left the conference. A key action area for members was to test tangibles with senior university colleagues, including directors of finance, especially around the changes to the VAT rules for shared services models.

COLLABORATE! members were also aware of the need to get the involvement of staff from contributing institutions. This has been made possible with the setting up of the NC Steering Group and the work of the strands which are engaging a range of staff. The team was also very aware of not duplicating the effort of work being done elsewhere and this shaped the NC work plan. Not all NC members immediately warmed to the CA approach: 'the Change Academy is a bit warm and fluffy and accountants would start in a different place' and 'we need to move quickly to meet external drivers and identify quick wins' and 'Shared Services hits all the political and practical drivers' (comments from an NC meeting).

The team gave expertise freely outside the 'normal' way of working, leading to some interesting comparisons and abstraction, for example conceiving the change using metaphors. Debate and discussion was robust and without prejudice; it felt liberating to think 'outside the box'. My role as team leader was to help create the conditions for free thought while working with the CA experts. This was needed to provide checks and balances for the group, as the whole thing felt destabilizing at times. On the basis that more options are generated by the use of the CA techniques, and that the uncertainty felt by the team in the early stages had developed into firm plans by the end, the model appears transferable to other change situations and to other problem-solving contexts. The rich pictures that were created, the creative thinking that emerged and the collaborative tools that were tried out brought out new meaning that then led to deeper questions and more divergent thinking than would otherwise have been achieved. By the end of the CA Conference, having spent dedicated time together, the team was functioning as a mature unit.

Conclusions

By collaborating and sharing across the north of England, universities can enhance their services to students and staff for a sustainable cost. There is further potential for the NC to provide savings *and* create competitive advantage for the region, of particular importance in the current economic climate. Its success will assist academic libraries to meet the current political agenda and demands from parent institutions, maximizing the potential for shared services now and in the future.

Gaining the necessary support at university level and staff acceptance for shared approaches is not to be underestimated, and the team is actively working with relevant external agencies on the project work strands. All members of the COLLABORATE! project team have benefited from active thinking techniques and problem-based emphasis, and have forged even stronger connections during the process. The level of trust needed for collaborations and the importance of the quality of those relationships for partnership working is also a learning point and future work will concentrate on both the business side of COLLABORATE! and the strategic gain of working with diverse sets of institutions.

So far the plans are embryonic, and to some extent aspirational. Also the financial environment for some institutions has eased, which means they are currently less concerned with saving money. Taking part in the CA has enabled ideas to be both nurtured and tested, releasing the actions required to tackle a complex change across a number of very different institutions. Taking a collaborative approach is therefore seen as the best way to unlock that creativity as well as being the objective of the change itself. Herein lies the transformative potential of the collaboration paradox – using these variances actively to engender ambition and engage staff in the partner organizations to be part of the change, as seen through the professional lens of librarianship.

It is argued that during times of uncertainty more ways of thinking about change are needed to reveal viable options and models, which inevitably mean self-knowledge and management of more complex relationships inside and outside the organization. Collaboration is no longer a value-added activity; it is core to our institutions, our libraries and our professional practice.

References

Adamson, V., Bacsich, P., Chad, K., Kay, D. and Plenderleith, J. (2008) JISC and SCONUL Library Management Study: an evaluation and horizon scan of the current library management systems and related systems landscape for UK higher education, Sero Consulting Ltd with Glenaffric Ltd and Ken Chad Consulting Ltd, www.jisc.ac.uk/media/documents/programmes/resourcediscovery/lmsstudy.pdf.

Blunden-Ellis, J. (1994) The Consortium of Academic Libraries in Manchester (CALIM):

strategic and development planning of a new consortium. In Helal, A. H., Weiss, J. W. (eds), *Resource Sharing: new technologies as a must for universal availability of information*, Universitätsbibliothek Essen.

Bulpitt, G. (ed.) (2012) *Leading the Student Experience: super-convergence of organisation, structure and business processes*, Series 3, Publication 5, Leadership Foundation for Higher Education, www.lfhe.ac.uk/publications/index.cfm/S3-05.

Business, Innovation and Skills Committee (2011) *Government Reform of Higher Education, Twelfth Report*, Business, Innovation and Skills Committee, www.publications.parliament.uk/pa/cm201012/cmselect/cmbis/885/88505.htm.

Curtis, G. (2011) *Academic Libraries of the Future, final report*, British Library, Joint Information Systems Committee (JISC), Research Information Network (RIN), Research Libraries UK (RLUK) and Society of College, National and University Libraries (SCONUL), www.sconul.ac.uk/topics_issues/LoF/LotFFinalreport.pdf.

Davies, R. (2011) 'One of You Can Cut the Cake; the Other Picks the First Slice': routes to consider how to selfishly improve academic library delivery through shared services, *New Review of Academic Librarianship*, **17** (2), 259–65.

Department for Business, Innovation and Skills (2010) *Securing a Sustainable Future for Higher Education: an independent review of higher education funding and student finance*, (the Browne Report), www.bis.gov.uk/assets/biscore/corporate/docs/s/10-1208-securing-sustainable-higher-education-browne-report.pdf.

Department for Business, Innovation and Skills (2011) *Higher Education: students at the heart of the system*, White Paper, Cm 8122, www.bis.gov.uk/assets/biscore/higher-education/docs/h/11-944-higher-education-students-at-heart-of-system.pdf.

European Commission (2011) *Communication from the Commission 'Horizon 2020 – The Framework Programme for Research and Innovation'*, Commission Staff Working Paper, Executive Summary of the Impact Assessment, http://ec.europa.eu/research/horizon2020/pdf/proposals/horizon_2020_impact_assessment_report_executive_summary.pdf.

Harper, R. and Corrall, S. (2011) Effects of the Economic Downturn on Academic Libraries in the UK: positions and reflections in mid 2009, *New Review of Academic Librarianship*, **17** (1), 96–128.

Higher Education Funding Council for England (HEFCE) (n.d.) VAT Cost-Sharing Exemption, www.hefce.ac.uk/whatwedo/lgm/efficiency/shared/vat.

Higher Education Library Technology Group (n.d.) Wiki: SCONUL Shared Services, http://helibtech.com/SCONUL_Shared_Services.

HM Treasury, (2010) *Spending Review 2010*, press notices, www.hmtreasury.gov.uk/spend_sr2010_press.htm, accessed 7 May 2012.

Joint Information Systems Committee (JISC) and Society for College, National and University Libraries (SCONUL) (n.d.) *Shared ERM Requirements Project*, http://sconulerm.jiscinvolve.org/wp.

Jubb, M. (2010) Challenges for Libraries in Difficult Economic Times: evidence from the UK, *LIBER Quarterly*, **20** (2), 132-51, http://liber.library.uu.nl/index.php/lq/article/view/7983.

Kidd, T. (2010) The View from the UK: the economic crisis and serials acquisitions on an offshore island, *Serials Librarian*, **59** (3/4), 384-93.

Monk, A. and Howard, S. (1998) The Rich Picture: a tool for reasoning about work context, *Interactions*, March/April, 21-30.

Nicholas, D. et al. (2010) The Impact of the Economic Downturn on Libraries: with special reference to university libraries, *The Journal of Academic Librarianship*, **36** (5), 376-82.

Pittilo, M. (2005) Learning to Accomplish Difficult Change: the role of the Change Academy, *Academy Exchange*, **1**, 10-12.

Quality Assurance Agency for Higher Education (QAA) (2012) *UK Quality Code for Higher Education: a brief guide*, www.qaa.ac.uk/Publications/InformationAndGuidance/Pages/quality-code-brief-guide.aspx.

RCUK (2011) *Efficiency 2011-15: ensuring excellence with impact*, Research Councils UK, www.rcuk.ac.uk/Publications/policy/Pages/Efficiency2011.aspx.

Seel, R. (2006) *Liquid Café*, www.new-paradigm.co.uk/liquid_cafe.htm.

Student Charter Group (2011) *Final Report*, www.bis.gov.uk/assets/biscore/higher-education/docs/s/11-736-student-charter-group.pdf.

Universities UK (2011) *Efficiency and Effectiveness in Higher Education: a report by the Universities UK Efficiency and Modernisation Task Group*, the Diamond Report, www.universitiesuk.ac.uk/Publications/Pages/EfficiencyinHigherEducation.aspx.

6 Leadership skills for collaboration: future needs and challenges

Sue Roberts, CEO and State Librarian, State Library of Victoria, Australia
Rachel Esson, Associate Director (Library Academic Services), Victoria University of Wellington, New Zealand

Introduction

This book explores the changing context of public services, and more specifically higher education, arguing that collaboration is the critical issue for the ongoing transformation and success of libraries, learning environments and learning services. This chapter explores these new demands on the people who work, and who potentially will work, in such services. Its central argument is that leadership development *for collaboration*, rather than leadership in general, is the single biggest issue and the single greatest lever for success in the future. Leadership and leaders at all levels are required when working across boundaries and when working in an increasingly diverse environment. This chapter explores this challenging issue in a global context, a context that demands increased flexibility when collaborating with diverse professional groups and where the boundaries of territory and service delivery become increasingly permeable. It will explore and provide models to help us consider these skills, attributes and behaviours indicating that certain approaches are transferable, transformational and sustainable across many kinds of libraries and learning environments. It will also discuss the significance of diversity and difference for leadership and suggest ways in which we can develop as individuals and as organizations in order to ensure effective collaboration and boundary crossing.

The leadership context: general observations

Several authors (including several of the contributors to this volume) have proposed that leadership is fundamental to the present and future development of library and information services - across all sectors - and to the future of public services in general. Yet this obsession with leadership, which pervades all aspects of our lives, conveys a disillusionment both with leaders in the current and recent global context and with models of leadership (Sinclair, 2007). There has been a cynicism and scepticism towards political and business leaders as we ask 'Has leadership failed? Or worse, is it simply absent?' (Walsh, 1994, 24); this has been exacerbated during the global financial crisis of the 21st century. The literature illustrates how much people and organizations expect from their leaders (see Kouzes and Posner, 2003), yet how often those expectations are not met.

It is useful to consider briefly how we conceive of 21st-century leadership and how theories of leadership have changed over the decades. The main trends can be summarized as:

- *trait spotting:* often referred to as 'the great man theory', which supposes that leaders are born, not made
- *style counselling:* based on the view that individuals can be developed as leaders (see Likert's four systems of leadership, 1961)
- *context fitting:* based on the view that leadership is context specific and therefore leaders adapt their behaviour as necessary with multiple choices including having, at different times, to *tell, sell, be participative* or *delegate*
- *21st-century leadership:* based on the view of a 21st-century leader as someone who has the right traits and style and can also adapt to context. Effective leadership is therefore seen as a process created by an individual (the 'learning leader') rather than dependent on their qualities (Hooper and Potter, 2001).

Two theories have also emerged strongly out of the 21st-century leadership model. *Shared leadership* is the concept that, in contrast to the heroic individual, leadership is across and within teams and shared by different members of staff. *Collaborative leadership*, which is this chapter's topic, is an emerging body of theory that focuses on the leadership skills and attributes needed to deliver results across organizational boundaries. Kanter (1994) talked of leaders who realize that some things cannot be controlled by formal systems but require a dense web of interpersonal connections. Since the 1990s we have seen the rapid escalation in the complexity and inter-connectedness of the world we live in, mainly due to the impact of the democratization of information and power, which has pushed collaboration to the fore in all parts of our lives. Social networking, crowd-sourcing and collaborative online spaces are some examples of this change, also confirmed by authors in Chapters 1 and 7. Ibarra and Hansen (2011) ask 'Are you a collaborative leader?' and urge leaders to shed the command-and-control style in favour of empowerment and the embracing of differences. Archer and Cameron (2008) highlight that getting value from difference is at the heart of the collaborative leader's task, while Abele (interviewed by Joni, 2012) talks of leaders who can deal with people who represent a diversity of expertise, experiences, cultures, ages and geographies. There is even a Google app for Android that helps you measure how much of a collaborative leader you are!

The leadership context: observations on higher education

This edited collection describes a professional context that demands working across professional and organizational boundaries, with, for example, mixed-mode roles, new departments created by super-convergence, and significant shared services in higher education and the public sector more widely, as described in Chapter 10. This is also within a context of constant and rapid change. Consequently, 'this new environment will have greater ambiguity and uncertainty, and many if not all aspects of leadership (e.g. strategy development) will require a more collaborative approach to leadership. The model of effective leadership in the future will be one of encouraging environments that unlock the entire organization's human asset potential' (Hernez-Broome and Hughes, 2004, 28).

The convergence of many different student-facing services and the evolution of university-wide holistic models is one example of the changing context that requires collaborative leadership. At its widest level, the holistic approach refers to a collaborative method applied to student support involving all staff at an institution. Strategies aiming to educate the whole student are now prevalent across the sector (Weaver, 2008; Bulpitt, 2012). The theoretical basis for this approach is based upon the argument that if support mechanisms are to address the 'whole' student, institutions need to build contacts between staff with the relevant expertise to provide this support.

The forces influencing the shift towards holistic student-support strategies can also be seen at play more broadly across the higher education sector, leading to increasingly holistic strategies for learning, teaching and research and the services that enable them. This has led to what is often termed the 'convergence' of services and roles in many higher education institutions (see Chapter 9). The notion of convergence is particularly prevalent in the literature on library and information services, with an emphasis on convergence between libraries and technology services (in the 1990s), but this has taken on new, more inclusive and complex meaning in the context described above. Specific drivers for this ongoing convergence have been identified in the literature as:

- rapid technological changes bringing roles and services closer together
- new affinities between groups of staff

- acknowledgement that services had to break away from rigid hierarchies and traditional modes of practice
- a new focus on the learner and services based on their needs and not structural and organizational concerns.

Many barriers can stand in the way of good collaborative efforts of this kind in the university setting. Cook and Lewis (2007) have identified the following:

- *Staff Attitudes* are by far the biggest barrier. Attitude shifts present a major challenge and one that requires a shift in thinking from individualistic approaches to holistic ones across the university as a whole.
- *History* can dictate that the way things have been determines what is expected, and this can become a *habit* that is hard to break. Simply because we haven't perhaps had a history of collaboration doesn't mean it is not worth a try.
- *Different cultures* can exist in the university setting. These can be between academic staff in different subject areas and between student or administrative staff and their academic colleagues. Crossing the border of these cultures can be daunting but enriching at the same time.
- *Communication* is the key but as universities get larger and workloads increase the opportunity and ability to communicate across usual barriers can become more difficult.
- *Autonomy* of individual groups, schools, disciplines or units can also act as a barrier to improving cross-collaboration.

We would add that the absence of highly effective and transformative leadership, focused on a clear vision, will also be a major barrier. Collaborative leadership, therefore, is the primary enabler that will counter these barriers. We will now explore the skills and behaviours that can form part of collaborative leadership in action.

Leadership skills and behaviours

Much of the literature about leadership in the library and information context provide lists of attributes and behaviours that if displayed will enable effective leadership (Parsons, 2004). In the current environment of advanced information technology, increasing diversity, the push to do more with less and to demonstrate the effectiveness of services, lists of attributes are no longer enough to guide us in the development of effective leadership. What is required is a model that will outline how the necessary skills and attributes can be implemented to create the best possible environment for effective collaboration to occur.

There is general agreement that the key attributes for successful leadership are not limited to a set of competencies but rather include the ability to be self-reflective and have good emotional intelligence. Leadership undoubtedly starts from within and is an 'inner game'. Self-reflection and emotional intelligence are particularly important when leading for collaboration because these attributes enable leaders to deal effectively with changes such as flattened hierarchies, advanced technological transformation, political agendas and increased diversity. Unhelpfully, many academics libraries and academic institutions are still relatively hierarchical in structure and although this is changing it has not changed as quickly as in other institutions and sectors. As Young (2007) predicts, library organizational structures, frequently unchanged for decades, will be increasingly flattened and streamlined. We consequently require leaders who can thrive within this new context.

This streamlining is necessary to create the environment for collaboration and partnerships within and external to higher education institutions. This flattening of structures requires leaders to interact and build relationships with a wider range of people than ever before and in a context of greater shared responsibility and shared leadership.

> Much has been written about partnerships and collaboration between and among libraries, but these relationships must first apply to the library staff and be present throughout the organisation.
>
> (Hernon and Rossiter, 2007, 165)

Information technology is another driver that has obviously had a disruptive impact – opening up possibilities and destabilizing existing models – on leadership hierarchies. Staff at any level have access to leaders via e-mail and social media, and indeed can become leaders and influencers through their own use of the latter.

The development of political understanding and the ability to function in a political environment is particularly important when building collaborative partnerships. This includes being politically strategic and knowing when preserving the relationship is more important than the desired outcome. Increasingly, leadership is about building relationships and developing collaborative approaches to deliver the best possible outcomes for stakeholders and customers.

Libraries will need to develop leaders from within their teams and to be explicit about the values and behaviours that are expected from those leaders. The shift from heroic individual to shared leadership means that 'Most organisations will not need the "Lone Ranger" type of leader as much as a leader who can motivate and coordinate a team-based approach' (Hernez-Broome and Hughes, 2004, 28).

Leading in diverse organizations

Earlier in the chapter we discussed how organizations are becoming increasingly diverse and that this has implications for leadership skills for collaboration. It has been recognized for some time that both staff and students in universities are becoming more diverse; this can be seen as a result of globalization and of universities' strategies to attract increasing international students and the best international scholars. We now live and work in a global marketplace. Changes in demographics in many countries mean that there is more diversity. For example,

- 2012 US census figures show that for the first time in US history minority births make up more than half of all births (US Census Bureau, 17 May, www.census.gov/newsroom/releases/archive)
- 2011 Australian census figures reveal that one in four Australians is born overseas with Hinduism the fastest growing religion (Australian Bureau of Statistics, 22 June, www.abs.gov.au/census).

At a university level, taking Victoria University of Wellington, New Zealand, as an example, we can also see increasing diversity. In 2010 a total of 22,310 students were enrolled. Of these,

- 46% were male
- 54% were female
- 19,803 were domestic students
- 2507 were international students
- 1966 were Māori students
- 1154 were Pacific students.

Recognition and awareness are key to building an understanding of cultures and different approaches to leadership. This can be described as *cultural intelligence.*

The following leadership attributes have been identified as being endorsed across cultures: encouraging, positive, motivational, confidence building, dynamic and foresighted. On the other hand, being a loner, non-cooperative, ruthless, non-explicit, irritable and dictatorial were seen as negative facets of leadership (Conger and Hunt, 1999, cited in Alvolio et al., 2003).

Further, the work of Avolio et al. (2003) highlights that although general patterns of leadership are similar across cultures, specific behaviours and attitudes expressed by leaders appear to differ across cultures. Collaborative leadership and leaders must be mindful of these differences and adapt to differing perspectives. Undoubtedly, increased diversity will require leaders in the higher education sector and beyond to possess a cultural intelligence characterized by tolerance, empathy and co-operativeness to appreciate differences among followers and collaborators.

Alire (2007) argues that it is not enough for leaders to empower the minorities in their organizations; they also have to develop them as leaders. It takes leaders who are very self-confident, who truly value diversity, who respond to minorities' needs and concerns, and who put the organizational mission and goals above their personal ones. It is not sufficient for leaders to be committed to diversity, they must turn that commitment into effective action and develop a record of success - nurturing the development of the minority and other staff members.

Within their organizations, leaders should also work with minority individuals and help them in their professional development. This should include supporting staff development programmes that will allow minority staff to move up within their organizations. The managerial leader should not wait for the minority employees to approach them. Leaders generally have a sense of who has great potential for leadership development. Consequently they should be proactive, and encourage and support minority employees to consider leadership development possibilities. More specifically, they should nominate them for leadership development programmes.

Leadership at all levels

The concept of collaborative leadership clearly resonates with, and supports, the idea of leadership at all levels in an organization. Where hierarchies are less clear, more leaders without positional power are likely to emerge. Roberts and Rowley (2008) also emphasize that, in this dynamic environment, leaders at all levels use their influence to lead and motivate others, to implement change, to lead teams and to shape values and culture. Leadership through influencing - rather than positional and traditional power - can therefore be viewed as a critical part of collaboration. Individuals must move from being 'judgers' to being 'learners' to be truly influential and collaborative, acknowledging that there will be many instances when to 'give something up' is for the greater good and to cede power is powerful in itself.

The literature on influencing often focuses on techniques that require us to be chameleons. Burton and Dalley (2010) provide a different model, which begins with understanding who you are and what you stand for. The model is represented in Figure 6.1 overleaf.

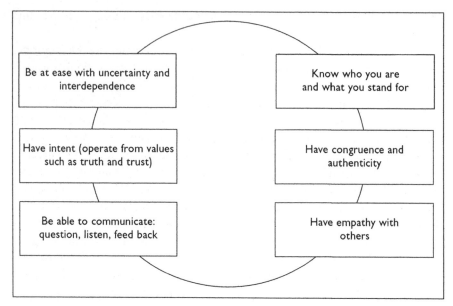

Figure 6.1 *Leadership model (Burton and Dalley, 2010)*

This model puts the leader personally at the centre of any collaboration, as influencing is deeply personal, stemming from 'who you are and what you stand for', which in itself creates authenticity and congruence (what you see on the outside reflects what is on the inside). The model then connects the personal with empathy for others, the basis for building rapport, which is developed through highly effective communication. The final two aspects of the model are 'intent', which relates to the purpose of the relationship, the goals being pursued, and the need to be at ease with uncertainty. We infer from this that the power of flexibility and the ability to adapt and compromise in any situation is crucial. This is particularly important in the context of influencing as part of collaboration; the collaboration itself and the agreed joint goals have to be the priority, more critical than an individual position or viewpoint.

Authentic leadership

As highlighted above, authenticity (which we define as understanding yourself and then behaving and communicating in ways that are congruent with this) is the foundation of influencing, and influential leadership; further, we argue that authenticity is the cornerstone of collaborative leadership. Authentic leadership recognizes that all leaders, whatever their role, age and background, are on a leadership journey. Authentic leadership is progressed through self-awareness, self-acceptance, authentic actions and relationships, while remaining cognizant of your own vulnerabilities (Luthans and Avolio, 2003). It is therefore very much an 'inner journey' and requires ongoing commitment to self-development and growth. Theorists in this field suggest that authentic leaders:

- are highly self-aware – first know yourself and lead yourself
- have clearly defined and strongly articulated values
- are consistent in what they say and how they behave
- have ongoing drive and motivation towards natural goals
- have the ability to harness followers.

The challenges for individuals wishing – or needing – to develop as collaborative leaders are therefore significant, especially as the contexts and organizations in which we work are not necessarily fertile grounds for collaborative approaches. We suggest that leadership models for collaboration can be helpful for practitioners seeking to lead across boundaries and can provide guidance for the development of a longer-term strategic view despite uncertainties and ambiguity in the environment.

Leadership models for collaboration

There are many leadership models in the literature – although few, if any, that demonstrate a model of collaborative leadership. We would like to explore models through the lens of collaboration as well as suggest a possible model for collaborative leadership. The example in Figure 6.2 on the next page is the Simmons Leadership Model for the Information Profession.

Unpacking the leadership areas identified in Figure 6.2 illustrates the synergies within this model and with the issues discussed in this chapter regarding collaborative leadership:

- *Transformation:* Visioning, energizing and stimulating a change process that coalesces communities, patrons and professionals around new models of managerial leadership.
- *Accomplishment:* Translating vision and strategy into optimal organizational performance. Accomplishment can also be defined as competence.
- *People:* Creating an organizational climate that values employees from all backgrounds and provides an energizing environment for them. It also includes the leader's responsibility to understand his or her impact on others and to improve his or her capabilities, as well as the capabilities of others.

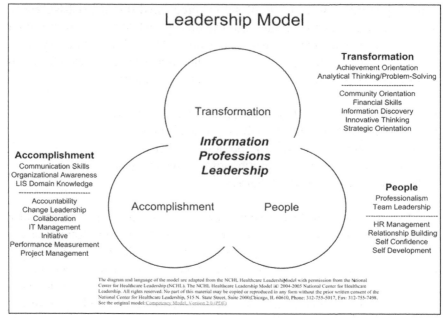

Figure 6.2 *Simmons Leadership model for the Information Profession*
(www.simmons.edu/gslis/docs/phdmlip_models_new_permission.pdf)
(Reprinted and used with permission from the National Center for Healthcare
Leadership (www.nchl.org), Chicago, IL., 1700 W. Van Buren, Suite 126B,
Chicago, IL, 60612, USA; reprinted with permission from the Graduate School of
Library and Information Science, Simmons College, USA.)

This model usefully presents the individual attributes required for leadership, especially in leading others. However, it does not consider the contextual nature of leadership and what is required in an increasingly collaborative environment. We therefore present in Figure 6.3 a collaborative leadership model that builds on these attributes while placing them in a collaborative environment. It is represented as a web to reflect the realities and complexities of collaboration and the other themes and issues explored in this chapter.

A case study from the University of Victoria, Wellington, New Zealand, illustrates the model in practice.

Case study: creating a Campus Hub through collaborative leadership

Between 2009 and 2013 Victoria University of Wellington (New Zealand) undertook an ambitious project to develop a Campus Hub. The Campus Hub aims to maximize new build and reorganize and redevelop existing spaces, to revitalize and reconnect the campus at its Kelburn location. At the centre of this

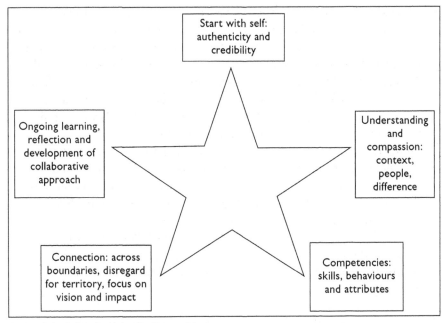

Figure 6.3 *Collaborative leadership model*

redevelopment is a renovated academic library that interlinks and integrates with social learning spaces, a range of student services, student union activities and retail. The project has significant strategic potential to make a long term impact on the student and staff experience and on the delivery of services. It should also be noted that this project reflects the international interest in holistic and shared services; there are many examples of campus or student hubs or centres in the tertiary sector globally. (See Chapter 8 for a description of the Saltire Centre, Glasgow Caledonia University, UK, an early leader in this field.)

Given the scope of the project there are many stakeholders and no one clear leader. Even more significantly, the stakeholders involved are not aligned structurally so there is no natural hierarchy. These stakeholders include: Facilities Management, IT Services, the Library, Student Academic Services, the Students Association and Faculties. The project is not simply a facilities project, a library project or a student services project; it is all of these and more. The potential for territoriality and turf warfare was a concern from the outset and was discussed openly and deliberately during the key phases. The Project Control Group consists of representatives from each of the stakeholder groups and the following approaches and strategies were put in place to maximize collaboration and minimize tensions:

- A focus on a shared vision and the benefits of the end result: the impact of the new concept and facility was constantly referred to, enabling a focus on the endgame rather than the difficulties of making it happen. This vision was shared and was greater than any individual- or service-specific goals.
- A pragmatic willingness to compromise and find solutions that would serve the vision: at different stages each partner was prepared to 'give up' something, for example the amount of space for certain activities, design preferences and the timings of aspects of the project.
- An understanding that different aspects of the project required different leadership and skills sets; one example is that the development of the service delivery model for the new space was led by the Library but was based on a strong collaborative implementation group that involved Student Academic Services, Faculties and IT Services.
- Everyone involved accepted their roles as champions for the project and appreciated the need to have shared leadership and shared ownership, particularly when representing the project across the university and externally.

The Campus Hub will be opened and operationalized in early 2013. The collaborative leadership demonstrated at its inception and throughout the project has not been without its tensions. Staff at different levels and across the many stakeholder groups have been involved and have provided leadership for the diverse aspects of the project and at different times. This shared and collaborative leadership will certainly be required on an ongoing basis to ensure success in the delivery and also the refinement of the model.

Leadership development for true collaboration

This final section focuses on career and personal development, both what we can and must do as organizations and as individuals. This chapter has already highlighted that leadership begins from within and is built on authenticity. Barrett takes this idea and combines the individual and organizational development using the theme of evolution:

> Three stages of development – learning how to become viable and independent, learning how to bond to form group structures, and learning how to cooperate to form a higher order entity – are the three universal stages of evolution.
>
> (Barrett, 2010, 19)

His model for leadership development stems from this concept and he argues that the five evolutionary characteristics listed below have been responsible for four billion years of evolution:

- adaptability - speed and resilience
- continuous learning - memory/logic
- ability to bond - compatibility/trust
- ability to co-operate - alignment/empathy
- ability to handle complexity - internal and external (Barrett, 2010, 66).

We see this model as being particularly pertinent to collaborative leadership and as a framework for dealing with ambiguity and uncertainty inherent in the models previously described.

A great deal has been written on leadership development opportunities including coaching, mentoring, programmes, experiential learning and so on. We do not want to replicate that here; rather we would like to present some opportunities for reflection - at an individual and organizational level - that are drawn from the models and discussion we have presented.

At an individual level:

- How can you deepen your connection to yourself? This will leverage your impact on the world by you becoming even more authentic and focused on your mission.
- How can you develop your compassion? Again, compassion must start with yourself and be applied to others.
- How can you widen your perspective, aiming to continually widen your understanding of difference?
- How can you assess your capacity for working with other people?
- How can you continuously challenge your own assumptions, and also the assumptions of others? As Barrett states, 'get beyond your attachment to being right and seek out what is true' (Barrett, 2010, 241).

We would also argue that most of this development needs to be undertaken through work on the self, and also through greater exposure to different contexts and people.

At an organizational level:

- How can we create conducive cultures in organizations for effective collaboration?
- How can we develop shared leadership, and also shared leadership across cultures, professional groups and distance?

- How can we create a culture that challenges assumptions and takes a holistic view?
- How can we develop a diverse organization and a workforce that celebrates difference?
- How can we create compelling visions for change, facilities and services that will unify diverse individuals and groups, and that will require collaborative leadership for their success?

In continuously developing and answering these questions we expose ourselves to personal challenge, reflection and development ensuring the sustainability of our leadership profile as true collaborators benefiting our current and future clients, our organizations and our profession.

Conclusions

We have deliberately not discussed particular professional skills sets in this chapter as we believe that, in an increasingly collaborative context, these will become less and less relevant. The willingness to work across boundaries, to give up territory and long-held assumptions, the desire to truly understand and empathize with others and the ability to embrace difference will be the attributes and beliefs that set collaborative leaders apart. As individuals, teams and organizations we must work to get the balance right between 'control, humility and attribution' (Joni, 2012). Wright (2010) identified 15 predictions about leadership of the future, which included several that resonate with the thinking in this chapter:

- The single, autocratic individualistic leader style will give way to a more facilitating, enabling leader who shares leadership widely and openly.
- Leaders will understand themselves better than ever before.
- Emotional intelligence, interpersonal skills and diversity management will become increasingly important.
- Leadership power will be spread throughout (especially down) the new, flatter organizations.

In a world based on so many interdependencies, success is increasingly based on the ability to collaborate. To thrive in this environment we must continue to explore and question notions of leadership that are fixed and based on outdated assumptions. We must embrace ambiguity and complexity, letting go of the desire to know and control with absolute certainty. We must aim to develop our own path as individuals and organizations which fully embraces ongoing learning, diversity and true collaboration with others.

References

Alire, C. (2007) Diversity and leadership. In Hernon, P. and Rossiter, N. (eds), *Making a Difference: leadership and academic libraries*, Libraries Unlimited.

Archer, D. and Cameron, A. (2008) *Collaborative Leadership: how to succeed in an interconnected world*, Butterworth Heinemann.

Avolio, B., Sosik, J., Jung, D. and Berson, Y. (2003) Leadership models, methods and applications. In Borman, W. C., Ilgen, D. R. and Klimoski, R. J. (eds), *Handbook of Psychology, Vol. 12, Industrial and Organizational Psychology*, John Wiley and Sons.

Barrett, R. (2010) *The New Leadership Paradigm: a leadership development textbook for the twenty-first century*, Amazon Distribution.

Bulpitt, G. (2012) *Leading the Student Experience: super-convergence of organisation, structure and business processes*, Research Publications, Series 3, Publication 5, Leadership Foundation for Higher Education, www.lfhe.ac.uk/en/research-resources/publications/index..cfm/S3-05.

Burton, L. and Dalley, D. (2010) *Developing Your Influencing Skills: how to influence people by increasing your credibility, trustworthiness and communication skills*, Universe of Learning Ltd.

Conger, J. A. and Hunt, J. G. (1999) Overview Charismatic and Transformational Leadership: II. Taking stock of the present and future, *Leadership Quarterly*, **10**, 121–7.

Cook, J. H. and Lewis, C. A. (2007) *Student and Academic Affairs Collaboration: the divine comity*, National Association of Student Personnel Administrators (NASPA).

Hernez-Broome, G. and Hughes, R. (2004) Leadership Development: past, present, and future, *People and Strategy*, **27** (1), 24–32.

Hernon, P. and Rossiter, N (eds) (2007) *Making a Difference: leadership and academic libraries*, Libraries Unlimited.

Hooper, A. and Potter, J. (2001) *Intelligent Leadership: creating a passion for change*, Random House Business Books.

Ibarra, H. and Hansen, M. T. (2011) Are You a Collaborative Leader?, *Harvard Business Review*, July/Aug, **89** (7/8), 96–109.

Joni, S.-N. (2012) The Crucial Question for Collaborative Leadership: a conversation with John Abele of Boston Scientific, *Forbes Leadership Forum*, www.forbes.com/sites/forbesleadershipforum/2012/05/07/the-crucial-quest-for-collaborative-leadership-a-conversation-with-john-abele-of-boston-scientific.

Kanter, R. M. (1994) Collaborative Advantage: the art of alliances, *Harvard Business Review*, July/Aug, **72** (4), 96–109.

Kouzes, J. M. and Posner, B. Z. (2003) *Credibility: how leaders gain and lose it, why people demand it*, Jossy-Bass.

Likert, R. (1961) *New Patterns of Management*, McGraw-Hill.

Luthans, F. and Avolio, B. J. (2003) Authentic Leadership: a positive development approach. In Cameron, K. S., Dutton, J. E. and Quinn, R. E. (eds), *Positive Organisational Scholarship*, Barrett-Koehler.

Parsons, F. (ed.) (2004) *Recruitment, Training and Succession Planning in the HE Sector: findings from the HIMSS project*, University of Birmingham.

Roberts, S. and Rowley, J. (2008) *Leadership: the challenge for the information profession*, Facet Publishing.

Sinclair, A. (2007) *Leadership for the Disillusioned: moving beyond the myths and heroes to leading that liberates*, Allen and Unwin.

Walsh, J. (1994) The Time Global 100, *Time*, 4 December, 24.

Weaver, M (ed.) (2008) *Transformative Learning Support Models in Higher Education: educating the whole student*, Facet Publishing.

Wright, L. (2010) The leadership of the Future. In McKnight, S. (ed.), *Envisioning Future Academic Library Services: initiatives, ideas and challenges*, Facet Publishing.

Young, A. (2007) Gen-xers and Millennials Join the Library Express. In Hernon, P. and Rossiter, N. (eds), *Making a Difference: leadership and academic libraries*, Libraries Unlimited.

7 Knowing me . . . knowing you: the role of technology in enabling collaboration

Graham Stone and Dave Pattern, University of Huddersfield, UK

Acknowledgements
The authors would like to thank all the staff who took part in the projects described below, particularly Andrew Walsh and Alison Sharman for their assistance in putting together the sections on Lemon Tree and the Roving Librarian respectively.

Introduction
This chapter uses the University of Huddersfield as an example of how technology has allowed libraries of all kinds to work more collaboratively and analyses to what extent these developments have been successful. It focuses on the broad approaches that are being used via innovative technology and rich media to both reach and understand our customers, as well as how developments in the community (e.g. open data, social media, open publishing, repositories and shared services) have enabled the sharing, use and re-use of information, data and objects:

> Our job over the next five to ten years is to provide a way to access these valuable resources in an intuitive, easy to use one-stop shop, and not to be afraid of running a continual beta test where new services and functions can be added as and when necessary. To do this we need flexible, interoperable resource-discovery systems based on open source software. In addition, we must keep evaluating users' needs and reach out by adapting our systems to fit their requirements, rather than expecting them to come to us; indeed our very future depends on it.
> (Stone, 2009, 156)

The chapter examines a selection of projects that have been inspired by the use of technology and social media at the University of Huddersfield in order to enrich the student experience. These projects have either been borne out of collaboration or inspired by the spirit of collaboration and sharing with others over a period of ten years (Brook et al., 2002; Stone, Ramsden and Pattern, 2011a; JISC, 2008; Sero, 2009; Pattern et al., 2010; Copac, 2012). The chapter will show the importance of both collaboration and the sharing of data and will discuss this in the context of collaboration on a national scale, for which Huddersfield's Computing and Library Services (CLS) staff have a national and international reputation.

In 2007, JISC (Joint Information Systems Committee) (Anderson, 2007), reported on the implications of the development of Web 2.0 technologies for the UK higher and further education sector by discussing six key themes:

1   Individual production
2   Harness the power of the crowd
3   Data on an epic scale
4   Architecture of participation
5   Network effects
6   Openness.

JISC concluded that Web 2.0 technologies change the way some people act. The report (Anderson, 2007) also highlights the importance of using and preserving the data being generated by Web 2.0 (and the difficulties of accessing and preserving the 'hidden web') and the shift to user-centred design of Library 2.0 services which is taking place.

Many of the projects at Huddersfield have come from user-driven technology, building on the founding principles and practices of Web 2.0, and are based on user collaboration where the user acts as co-developer (Collins, 2012), in that the tools 'get better the more people use them' (O'Reilly, 2006). Huddersfield has been experimenting with social media tools for several years and has utilized usage data in a number of ways to encourage an element of serendipity in discovering resources. Some of the results of this work have led to other internal and external projects, some of which are described in this chapter.

Resource discovery

Why is Google so easy and the library so hard?   (Tenopir, 2009)

In recent years libraries and librarians have struggled to persuade users to move away from Google, seeing it as a direct competitor to traditional library resources. However, this raises an important question: why do users flock to Google and what can we learn from this? A factor in the success of companies such as Google, Amazon and Tesco PLC is that they work hard to collect and understand their customers' data to provide the services that users want, enhancing and simplifying resource discovery and adding value.

Enhancing resource discovery: understanding the data

> . . . many librarians do not have sufficient understanding of their users and, as a
> direct consequence, are facing serious problems.   (Nicholas, 2008, 1)

Initial work on understanding data at Huddersfield using Web 2.0 technologies in order to enhance resource discovery was centred on the library catalogue. Recommender services and usage logs were used to create additional features (Pattern, 2009). Owing to the nature of the catalogue's holdings, work had often focused on increasing the use of print resources. Typically this included features such as a keyword cloud on the front page displaying the most popular keywords of the last two days, a 'did you mean . . .' option and spell checker, which was introduced to counter the ongoing issue with search results that returned zero hits (this accounted for 23% of searches over one six-month period), instead providing a serendipity search, generating suggestions for the user by running the search against sites such as www.answers.com. These results are then compared against the catalogue to generate a series of potentially relevant keyword searches.

Further analysis of user activity within the library catalogue revealed that the word 'renew' was a common search in the catalogue. To aid the user, the message 'To renew items you currently have on loan, please click on the "My Account/Renewals tab"' now appears, which prompts the user to go to the correct option in the catalogue. A 'people who borrowed this also borrowed' option based on borrower history is also available and is a feature that users will be familiar with from sites such as Amazon.

In order to enrich the student experience when using the catalogue, further services based on usage data have also been implemented. This includes an in-house system, inspired by the Ex Libris bX recommender service (Ex Libris, 2011), which provides recommendations based on usage data for both books in the catalogue and e-journals using the 360 API (application programming interface) (Serials Solutions®, 2012a) from Serials Solutions®.

Trends in borrowing patterns cannot be directly attributed to these services; however, there is a noticeable increase in usage. Unique titles borrowed from the library jumped in 2006 after the first of these services were introduced. Perhaps more significantly, the average number of items borrowed per user also increased (see Figure 7.1 overleaf).

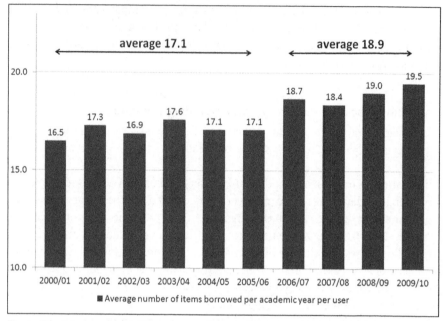

Figure 7.1 *Average number of items borrowed per academic year per user at the University of Huddersfield*

More recently work has been extended to include the new reading-list software MyReading (Pattern, 2011a), which includes a feature that exploits usage data to recommend wider reading. This initial work on usage data has been the basis for many of the collaborative projects undertaken by Huddersfield and its partners described later in the chapter.

Simplifying resource discovery: the Summon™ project

> These products present a new generation of resource discovery by attempting to provide the best bits of federated search while eliminating the downside.
>
> (Stone, 2009, 146)

Since 2009, a number of web-scale discovery systems have come to market. These systems move a step beyond the traditional federated-search products by creating a union index of harvested content direct from publishers and local library collections in order to make searching simple and fast (Gibson, Goddard and Gordon, 2009). Unlike federated search, web-scale discovery means that users no longer have to wait for the slowest resource to retrieve a search before all results are displayed, or to have to negotiate separate online resource platforms in order to find information. Summon™ is one such service.

In the summer of 2009, after a comprehensive review of the market, the University of Huddersfield became the first UK commercial adopter of Summon™ from Serials Solutions® (Stone, 2010). Huddersfield was followed by a number of other UK universities in purchasing Summon™, including Northumbria University. In 2009 Huddersfield and Northumbria Universities collaborated on a successful proposal entitled 'Simplifying resource discovery and access in academic libraries: implementing and evaluating Summon™ at Huddersfield and Northumbria Universities' or Summon4HN™ (Pattern et al., 2010), which was funded under the JISC Information Environment Programme 2009-11. The project aimed to create a case study report describing the selection, implementation and testing of Summon™ at both universities, drawing out common themes as well as differences, with suggestions for those intending to implement Summon™ and some ideas for future development (Thoburn, Coates and Stone, 2012).

Although Huddersfield and Northumbria implemented Summon™ at slightly different times, the two universities collaborated in assessing the support from Serials Solutions® and listed a number of recommendations for others planning their own implementation. Following implementation both universities worked together to devise a similar online survey and a common approach to running focus-group sessions. Feedback was also gathered from staff and students through formal training sessions. Data was collected to ascertain what users liked and did not like about Summon™ to gauge the impact of such a major cultural change to library systems and to improve training materials where necessary. Huddersfield and Northumbria produced marketing material which was then made available on the project blog for others to share. The final report detailed a number of recommendations for Serials Solutions®. Key points for effective practice for others planning to implement Summon™ were also described and these may impact on project planning and timescales for implementation at other universities (Thoburn, Coates and Stone, 2010).

One of the impacts of the collaboration between Huddersfield and Northumbria was the formation of the UK Summon™ User Group, which is now part of the wider Serials Solutions® User Group UK (Serials Solutions® User Group UK, n.d.); this user group, currently chaired by Huddersfield, meets twice a year, with one meeting in the north of England or Scotland and one in the south of England, in addition to the yearly Summon™ Camp Europe meeting that takes places after the UK Serials Group (UKSG) Conference (www.uksg.org). The group exists to share knowledge and experiences and regularly feeds back to Serials Solutions® with recommendations for enhancements and community developments, such as the Community wiki (Serials Solutions®, n.d.).

Adding value

> ... there is a continuing focus on the student experience and a desire that all
> students should achieve their full potential whilst studying at University.
>
> (Stone, Ramsden and Pattern, 2011c)

This chapter has discussed the use of data in order to improve the student experience; however, so far we have only seen anecdotal evidence that the library adds value (see Figure 7.1). Data, specifically library usage data, can also be used to understand student activities and show that the library has a real impact.

The Library Impact Data Project

> There is a statistically significant correlation across a number of universities
> between library activity data and student attainment.
>
> (Stone, Ramsden and Pattern, 2011a)

The Library Impact Data Project (LIDP) was developed from earlier work undertaken at Huddersfield (Goodall and Pattern, 2011; White and Stone, 2010a), which analysed the non/low use of library resources over a four-year period (2005 to 2009). The initial driver of this work came from a project looking at equality impact assessments. Library usage data, defined as the number of e-resources accessed, the number of book loans and the number of physical accesses to the library, was compared against student attainment. The initial work suggested a strong correlation between library usage and degree results obtained by students, notably with a significant underuse of library resources at both faculty/school and course level emerging as a factor. This evidence was presented at the 2010 UKSG Conference (White and Stone, 2010b). However, it was emphasized that the data did not in itself prove irrefutably a cause-and-effect relationship between library usage and student attainment. In addition, it was not known whether the Huddersfield findings would be substantiated when compared with those from other institutions.

As a result of this pioneering work, a number of universities approached Huddersfield in order to benchmark against the data results. In February 2011 the University of Huddersfield along with seven UK partners (University of Bradford, De Montfort University, University of Exeter, University of Lincoln, Liverpool John Moores University, University of Salford and Teesside University) successfully bid through the JISC Activity Data programme to:

> ... address common challenges such as:

- ensuring privacy,
- sharing data between systems and institutions,
- effective analysis,
- enabling reuse and developing or enhancing tools and services.

(JISC, 2011)

Projects under this call were asked to provide a hypothesis; in the case of the LIDP it was that

> There is a statistically significant correlation across a number of universities
> between library activity data and student attainment.

(Stone, Ramsden and Pattern, 2011a)

One of the greatest challenges of any collaborative project, especially one with such a limited timescale, is the ability to get all parties to share the same understanding of purpose to work together and provide deliverables at the right time. The project anticipated that there may be issues in collecting the data from the collaborators at an early stage, not least because of the short timescale of the project; this was seen as a significant risk. All potential partners were asked if they could provide at least two of the three measures of usage required as well as the student attainment data (see Figure 7.2) in a machine readable format (Stone, Pattern and Ramsden, 2011a).

Data Requirements for Project Partners
For a specific academic year (e.g. 2009/10), extract details for each graduating student

- academic year of graduation e.g. *2009/10*
- course title
- length of course in years
- type of course
- grade achieved
- school/academic department
- number of items borrowed from library
  - — either the total number borrowed by that student
  - — or separate values for each academic year
- number of visits to the library
  - — either the total number of visits by that student
  - — or separate values for each academic year
- number of logins to e-resources (or some other measure of e-resource usage)
  - — either the total number of logins made by that student
  - — or separate values for each academic year If you have other library usage data – e.g. number of library PC logins – please feel to include that in the extract.

Figure 7.2 *Data requirements (excerpt from Stone, Pattern and Ramsden, 2011a)*

Data provided from the partners was analysed, and the project successfully demonstrated that there is a statistically significant relationship between student attainment and two of the indicators: those of e-resources use (authentication logs) and book-borrowing statistics. This relationship has been shown to be true across all eight partners in the project that provided data for these indicators. Figure 7.3 shows a typical result from one of the project partners; figures are based on averages for each degree classification.

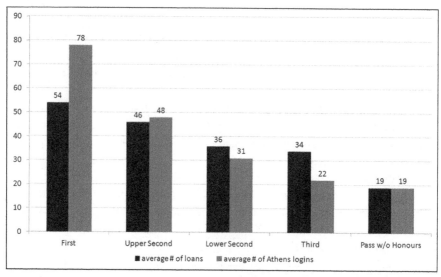

Figure 7.3 *Relationship between book loans/Athens (e-resources authentication) and student attainment (Stone, Pattern and Ramsden, 2011a)*

One area where a statistical significance was not found was for library gate entry data. The project partners attributed this to the fact that students enter the library building for a number of reasons, such as use of group study facilities, lecture theatres, cafés and social spaces, and to access student services, and that a student is just as likely to be entering the building for these reasons as to visit the library, which may or may not have an impact on their final grade.

Close collaboration by the partners throughout the project resulted in a number of important lessons being learned, for example one of the partners discovered that there was a local issue with the retention of data within the university. As a result, the project made a number of recommendations for other libraries to include forward planning for the retention of data. The LIDP used EZProxy and Athens authentication data to measure the number of times a student was logged into the university's e-resources. This data may not be as reliable as Counting Online Usage of Networked Electronic Resources (COUNTER) reports (www.projectcounter.org);

however, it was the only comparable data that can be collected and traced back to an individual. The project found that different institutions collect different data in this respect and some do not collect this data at all.

As noted above, a significant risk to the project was in getting eight universities to work to a common goal in a short space of time, and the success of the overall project was dependent on the contributions of all the partners, who made every deadline and in many cases provided additional information over and above the project's specification.

The project generated much interest from other universities in the UK, Europe, Australia and the USA. As a result the University of Huddersfield submitted a proposal for an extension to the original project and in December 2011 funding was approved to take this forward into Phase 2. Phase 2 will further exploit the data and investigate possible causal aspects that may influence usage and attainment. This investigation will help libraries make service improvements and provide better management information, thus refining decision-making and showing the value-added impact of academic libraries. Phase 2 of the project will use final percentage mark gained rather than degree classification to check for a correlation between usage and outcomes including mapping to demographic information, such as ethnicity, disability and country of domicile, for example overseas students' 'home' country, to understand usage patterns. In addition, the project is looking at information about students who dropped out of their course early (Stone, Collins and Pattern, 2012).

JISC has asked the project to conduct a feasibility study on the viability of a national shared service that involves collection and analysis of library impact data for all UK higher education (HE) libraries. Potentially this would ease the process of data collection and allow benchmarking to be undertaken by a central clearing house.

The LIDP is also liaising with other projects undertaking similar research, such as that being carried out at the University of Wollongong (Margie and Cox, 2010) and by Megan Oakleaf for the Association of College and Research Libraries (ACRL) (ACRL, 2010) in order to benchmark the findings. A more direct way to benchmark is the release of data under an Open Data Commons licence (Open Data Commons, n.d.) in order to encourage the sharing of '. . . potentially useful data to a much wider community and attaching as few strings as possible' (Pattern, 2008).

Shared data

The coolest thing to do with your data will be thought of by someone else.

(Walsh and Pollack, 2007)

One of the philosophies at Huddersfield is to share data where possible under an Open Data Commons licence. As part of the JISC TILE project (JISC, 2008), in 2008 Huddersfield released book circulation and recommendation data, which included over 80,000 titles derived from just under three million circulation transactions over a 13-year period. The data released covered two areas:

- Library circulation data: this breaks down the loans by year, by academic school and by individual academic courses. This data was primarily of interest to other academic libraries, and the relevant UCAS course codes were included to allow benchmarking (UCAS is the organization responsible for managing applications to HE courses in the UK, Universities and Colleges Admissions Service, www.ucas.ac.uk).
- User recommendation data: this is the data which drives the 'people who borrowed this, also borrowed . . .' suggestions in the library catalogue referred to earlier (Pattern, 2008).

The data, which was thoroughly aggregated and anonymized before release, went on to inspire the JISC Mosaic Project (Sero, 2009), which planned to 'investigate the technical feasibility and issues around exploiting data to assist resource discovery and evaluation in higher education'. Data in the Mosaic Project included circulation data from Huddersfield and others.

The LIDP also had the express aim of releasing all data from the project. After consultation with the partners the release of an anonymized set of data (Pattern, 2011b) was agreed under an Open Data licence. The data contains final grade and library usage figures for 33,074 students studying undergraduate degrees at the eight partner universities. In order to ensure complete anonymity for the partners they are listed as LIB1 to LIB8; subject disciplines at each university have been replaced by randomly generated identifiers (IDs) and some courses have been 'generalized' to remove elements that may identify the institution. A further output of the LIDP was a toolkit (Stone, Ramsden and Pattern, 2011b), which provides instructions for libraries on how to extract their own data in order to benchmark against the data described above. The toolkit discusses the extraction of the data and gives advice for statistical analysis and suggestions for further investigation. Phase 2 of the LIDP will build on the original toolkit as more data is extracted, in addition to releasing the new data under an Open Data Commons licence.

Another collaborative data project, the Copac Activity Data Project (CopacAD) (Copac, 2012), is adding to ten years' worth of circulation data from the University of Manchester by adding normalized data from Cambridge University, University of Lincoln, Sussex University and University of Huddersfield to build a recommender service using a web-based API. CopacAD aims to

> strengthen the existing business case for openly sharing circulation data to support
> recommendations, and will produce a scoping and feasibility report for a shared
> national service to support circulation data aggregation, normalization, and
> distribution for reuse via an open API.   (Copac, 2012)

Data code from the Summon4HN™ Project was also shared under Creative Commons licence for others to use as part of their implementation of Summon™ (Pattern et al., 2010).

Another form of collaboration through the use of data are the mashed library events, 'an un-conference' styled event centred on the use of data mash-ups in a library context, or 'bringing together interested people and doing interesting stuff with libraries and technology' (Balman, 2009). These events have been running since the original event in 2008 at Birkbeck College, UK, organized by Owen Stephens. Huddersfield hosted the second event, 'Mash Oop North', in 2009. These events aim to attract 'tech-savvy' librarians, developers and students and facilitate an environment where delegates can benefit from the opportunity to meet like-minded delegates and discuss and share data on topics such as information literacy, mobile technologies and Web 2.0. The 'un-conference' combines a networking event with pre-planned and lightning talks and can be highly unpredictable, but very creative (not dissimilar to the creative thinking process described in Chapter 5). Mashed library events since have been held all over the UK, such as MashSpa (aka 'Mash and Mashibility') and Pancakes and Mash.

A fundamental aim of using data collected either at the institutional level or via collaboration at library level is to improve the student experience by gaining a better understanding of students' needs. One such project at Huddersfield is the Roving Librarian Project. The project is further inspired by the findings of the LIDP and its predecessor, the non/low-use project (Goodall and Pattern, 2011), and by the collaboration work done in conjunction with the Students' Union as part of the Summon4HN™ Project, and is described next.

Roving Librarian

> Explor(ing) the possibility of using informal, mobile environments to interact with
> students and offer them on the spot information skills inputs.
>   (Sharman, 2011)

The original non/low-use library project revealed an underlying lack of use of the physical and electronic resources in the library across all academic schools (Goodall and Pattern, 2011). As many as 40% of full-time undergraduates did not visit the physical library during the length of their course. Although the LIDP did not find an overall statistical significance between student attainment and visits to the library, it did find significance between visits and higher and lower degrees (Stone, Pattern and Ramsden, 2011b). However, regardless of significance, students who do not visit the library are obviously missing out on the physical resources and also the training and support on offer. This training and support has traditionally been held in the library, either in induction or literature-searching sessions or via one-to-one appointments with library staff.

During the implementation of Summon™ a slightly different approach was taken, with a number of drop-in sessions being held outside the library, most notably in collaboration with the Students' Union. These sessions proved popular with students, but the staff who ran the sessions felt that the set up was rather 'cumbersome', as the laptop was slow to boot, required a desk to be set up and immediately formalized what was intended to be an informal situation. However, the drop-in sessions were considered very successful as, by leaving the confines of the library, staff were able to engage with students with little or no library experience in a more informal environment.

Roving Librarian received funding from the University of Huddersfield's Teaching and Learning Institute (TALI) (University of Huddersfield, n.d.) and takes its inspiration from work undertaken at the University of Queensland (Lister, 2007), which used a Roving Librarian equipped with a tablet to replace enquiry desk services. The project allowed librarians to answer questions and demonstrate services while on the move and to run drop-in sessions within buildings across campus. These drop-in sessions are advertised via e-mail and social media and provide support at the point of need. It is hoped that by raising staff and student awareness of library resources using mobile technology that more use will lead to higher achievement. Initial findings are that the project is proving successful in reaching students who may not necessarily enter the library.

Engaging library staff and users with new technologies

I have joined Twitter (which I hate to admit is a lot better than I thought it would be).
(Anon, 2011)

As described earlier in this chapter, Huddersfield has been experimenting with Web 2.0 technologies for a number of years by using a drip-feeding approach, both via the library catalogue for users and by using a variety of blogs and wikis for staff. This section will discuss how these technologies have been used to engage with staff and users at a more fundamental level. Owing to the very nature of social media, collaboration had been on a very informal level, often using the media itself to collaborate and discuss ideas.

Social media

> ... in the last ten years, social media have gone from a radical way of exploiting the networked promise of the internet to a routine part of many people's personal and professional lives.
> (Collins, 2012)

The drip-feeding approach has meant that while many library staff were using blogs and wikis, others were completely unfamiliar with such technologies. This apparent skills gap was the inspiration for Huddersfield's '25 Things for Computing and Library Staff' (Barrett et al., 2008). The course itself was based around the Learning 2.0 concept created by Helene Blowers (Blowers, 2006a), the then Technology Director at the Public Library of Charlotte and Mecklenburg County, USA. Learning 2.0 was aimed at encouraging public library staff to learn about the new and emerging Web 2.0 technologies. Blowers adopted a 'steal these ideas' approach by licensing the programme under Creative Commons, and around 500 libraries across the world have adapted the course (Blowers, 2006b). Huddersfield 'stole' ideas from two other programmes: Learning 2.0 @ Mac from McMaster University, Canada (McMaster University, 2007) and Library 23 Things from Murdoch University, Australia (Murdoch University, 2007), and also the work undertaken by Bobbi Newman, then at Missouri River Regional Library (Newman, 2011). In 2009, 25 Things at Huddersfield and Learning 2.0 at Imperial College London became the first two Library 2.0 programmes in UK HE (Barrett et al., 2009).

The idea for the follow-up '25 Research Things' course (Collins, Pattern and Stone, 2011) is a case study in collaboration and technology in itself. Initial discussions about the idea came about after a 'tweet-up' at the 2010 LIBER conference. This sparked a conversation about the then forthcoming UK Research Information Network (RIN) report on the take-up of social media and Web 2.0 tools and technologies within the research community (RIN, 2010). Huddersfield and the RIN collaborated in writing and delivering '25 Research Things', an innovative online learning programme which gave researchers a structured way to engage with selected Web 2.0 tools. The collaboration itself was done entirely via Google Docs, with the three authors not meeting for the first time together until after the course had started.

The course ran with two cohorts during 2010 to 2011 via a WordPress

(wordpress.org) blog. The 'thingers', ranging from first-year PhD students to professors, were given specific tasks, which encouraged them to take control of their learning through exploration and play. All participants established and maintained a blog of their own to report on their experiences with each tool. This helped to build a supportive community, with participants commenting on each other's blogs. As a result, they not only received peer support on the various tasks, but also began to understand the benefits of being part of an active online social network. A number of Web 2.0 tools were introduced each week around the themes shown in Table 7.1.

Table 7.1 *Themes covered in 25 Research Things*	
Themes	**Tool**
Blogs and RSS feeds	Wordpress Technorati Google Reader
Organizing your favourite content	Diigo LibraryThing Mendeley CiteULike
Social networks	Twitter Lanyrd LinkedIn
Sharing content you've created	SlideShare and Prezi Google Documents Creative Commons
Images	Flickr Mashups Online Image Generators
Play week	MyExperiment or arts-humanities.net Wikipedia
Audiovisual	YouTube Podcasts

All 'thingers' completed a survey before and after the course. The preliminary results of these surveys, along with analysis of the blogs, suggested that researchers found the course to be useful. For many, it increased their confidence in using Web 2.0 tools; many have also commented on the engaging and stimulating nature of the course, particularly its interactivity and structured learning.

Unfortunately, many participants did not make it beyond the first few weeks; more support at this stage from the 25 Research Things team may have been needed, including an initial face-to-face launch event. However, most of those who completed the course enjoyed it and felt it was pitched at the right level for their needs. In particular, they enjoyed reading each other's blogs – both to get a different perspective on the tools they were trying, and also to get to know other researchers at Huddersfield.

Observation of the blogs revealed that most researchers who finished the course said that there were some tools that they would continue to use and identified some that they did not find useful but might return to later. Many of the researchers also commented that being able to discriminate between the useful and less useful tools was very important. In this respect, the course broke down the somewhat daunting concept of Web 2.0 into different and more manageable techniques which can be adopted, or not, according to the researcher's individual needs. Even those participants who already had some experience with Web 2.0 tools found the course useful, either because it introduced them to tools they had not previously encountered, or because it gave them a dedicated framework to explore and experiment with the full capacities of services that they already used.

Researchers identified several ways that Web 2.0 tools would enhance their existing research processes, a point also mentioned in Chapter 1. These included: finding resources, managing references, showing ways of communicating findings, working with collaborators in other departments or institutions on articles and grant applications; and the potential value of Web 2.0 tools in building their professional networks, and in finding collaborators and possibly also new jobs. An unexpected outcome of the course was the potential for added value to teaching and learning, as many participants used ideas from the course with their students, such as CiteULike (www.citeulike.org) to compile reading lists, or Prezi (www.prezi.com) to deliver presentations. Others asked students to blog about their experiences on a work placement, for example.

Huddersfield and Imperial College London had remained in contact since the original 25 Things course in 2009. In May 2011, Imperial launched its own Web 2.0 course for researchers, entitled 'Blogs, Twitter, wikis and other web-based tools' (Imperial College, 2011). The course addressed many of the issues that the Huddersfield course encountered, such as the length of the course and its impact on the busy schedules of researchers. The Imperial model was much shorter with a minimum of six blog posts, including three compulsory elements and three optional elements. Looking to the future, Huddersfield plans to revisit the 25 Research Things course as part of a project on information literacy for researchers, which will roll out in 2013.

Lemon Tree

Why do we want to teach our users to be librarians?   (Pattern, 2009)

Lemon Tree (see Figure 7.4), like 25 Research Things, is designed to be a fun, innovative, low-input way of engaging students through new technologies and increasing use of library resources and therefore, final degree awards. It aims to increase usage via an easily adaptable social game-based e-learning platform to enhance the Huddersfield CLS environment. Lemon Tree focuses on students rather than on staff-intensive instruction and the traditional promotion of library resources. This allows sharing of the student experience of library resources by peers.

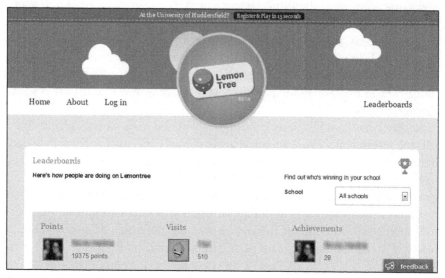

Figure 7.4 *Lemon Tree*

Lemon Tree (Running in the Halls, 2011) is another project that took part of its inspiration from the non/low-use project at Huddersfield (Goodall and Pattern, 2011). The project is a collaboration between CLS and Running in the Halls, the key collaborator being a former lecturer at Huddersfield, who based his Masters dissertation on innovative methods of interacting with the library. This project aims to increase usage of library resources using a custom, social game-based e-learning platform designed by Running in the Halls. This builds on previous ideas such as those developed at Manchester Metropolitan University to support inductions and information literacy (Whitton and Jones, 2009). In addition, Lemon Tree uses rewards systems similar to those used in location-based social networks such as Foursquare (foursquare.com).

As part of the project an evaluation of student perceptions of social game-based learning systems will be undertaken. In addition, the project intends to provide data to Phase 2 of the LIDP project in order to assess whether participation in Lemon Tree helped to increase student attainment through increased use of library resources. When registering, students sign terms and conditions that allow their student number to be passed to CLS. This allows CLS to track usage of library resources by Lemon Tree gamers versus students who do not take part. This data will then be anonymized and analysed as part of the LIDP.

Lemon Tree's primary objective is to improve student attainment through better use of library resources and engagement with new technologies. However, additional outcomes of the project are to provide a better awareness of how a social game-based learning approach may work across the University and the sector as a whole and to reduce staff time spent on library and computing inductions, thereby releasing valuable staff resource for other uses. It is expected that, if successful, other institutions would be interested in collaborating on further developments of the proposed system.

Collaboration at the national level

> ... there is potential for HEIs (Higher Educations Institutions) to secure sustainable efficiencies (including both economic benefits and service improvements) where they are not in direct competition. This is not just through sharing support functions, but through considering the wider range of areas where there is collaboration.
>
> (KPMG, 2006 3)

So far this chapter has looked at how the University of Huddersfield has used technology to collaborate with others to improve the student experience at a local level. This section will look at two further JISC projects, which are inspired by calls for collaboration and whose recommendations are aimed at the national level.

Huddersfield Open Access Publishing

> Open access publishing has arrived.
>
> (Bloomsbury Qatar Foundation Journals, 2011)

At the time of writing, open access (OA) is front-page news, On 2 May 2012, David Willetts, Minister of State for Universities and Science in the UK, addressed the Publishers Association annual general meeting regarding the government's commitment to OA: 'Opening up access to academic research will put more data and power in the hands of the people who pay for it' and maximize the impact and value of the UK research base (Willetts, 2012a, 2012b). In March 2012,

Research Councils UK (RCUK) released its draft policy (RCUK, 2012) on access to research outputs, clarifying that their definition of OA includes unrestricted use and reuse of content as allowed for under the Creative Commons Attribution (CC-BY) licence.

Huddersfield has been using the EPrints (www.eprints.org) platform for its institutional repository since 2006 (University of Huddersfield, 2012). Like many repositories, the aims of Huddersfield's institutional repository are twofold: to provide a complete record of the University's research outputs and to make as many of them available on OA as possible; currently around a third of outputs are available on OA (50% of those published since 2008), including PhD theses, conference papers, journal articles, book chapters and non-textual material such as artwork.

The institutional repository also provides data to the University's research information management system, which is an in-house system developed for the 2014 Research Excellence Framework (REF, www.ref.ac.uk) and funded through a number of successful JISC funding calls.

In 2011 the University relaunched the University of Huddersfield Press. The Press was investigating the possibility of supporting University journals and developed the Huddersfield Open Access Publishing (HOAP) Project (Stone et al., 2012), which aimed to develop a low cost, sustainable OA journal publishing platform using EPrints institutional repository software. The project was funded by JISC and led by CLS, in conjunction with the School of Education and Professional Development and the Research and Enterprise Directorate (see Figure 7.5).

Taking inspiration from an earlier project at the University of Glasgow (University of Glasgow, 2004), the HOAP project developed a platform to convert the peer-reviewed journal *Teaching in Lifelong Learning* (University of Huddersfield, 2009), from a print subscription model to an OA e-journal. A front-end was created for the journal with content being archived in the University repository. The creation of the journal landing pages (Figure 7.5) and the volume/issue pages is fully automated, enabling articles to be uploaded into the repository using existing workflows in just 30 minutes. The articles themselves maintain the standard repository branding linking back to the journal landing pages on the platform, aiding discovery via Google (Scholar) (scholar.google.co.uk/). Journals on the platform have been submitted to the Directory of Open Access Journals (Directory of Open Access Journals, 2012), which will enable the journals on the platform to be retrievable from resource discovery systems such as Summon™.

In order to disseminate its output and to encourage this sort of collaboration at other universities, the project developed a toolkit (Stone, 2011), which features sections on how to move to an OA model, setting up the landing pages and

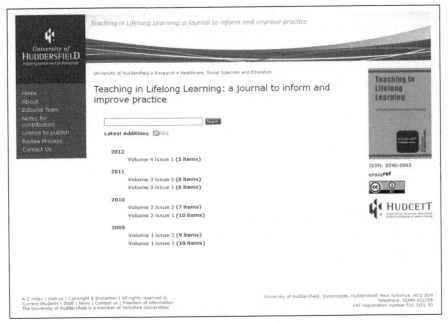

Figure 7.5 *Teaching in Lifelong Learning: a journal to inform and improve practice*

adding content, workflows and notes for contributors, including a licence to publish document.

The project was also keen initiate informal collaboration through social media by encouraging reader comments and ratings and social tagging as part of the publication process. Although this has been partly achieved through the bookmarks and sharing features of the existing repository, RSS feeds and automated tweets for new articles and through the project blogs and tweets, the project team wanted to go one step further by encouraging authors and readers to use social media by implementing the SNEEP (Social Networking Extensions for EPrints) suite of social networking extensions as part of the next release of EPrints (JISC, 2007). This will allow readers of the journal (and other repository content) to comment, tag and make notes once they log in.

The HOAP project concluded with a list of recommendations for the wider community around the agenda for national shared services. It is hoped that this project will help to encourage other universities to investigate publishing in-house journals for early-career researchers and undergraduates and perhaps pool resources by using the HOAP software as part of the EPrints Bazaar (EPrints, n.d.).

The UK HE sector has a rich history of collaboration through shared services at this level. Recently this has been led by work on shared services by SCONUL (the Society of College, National and University Libraries), which reported to the

Higher Education Funding Council for England (HEFCE) in late 2009 (SCONUL, 2010). The shared services agenda generated a lot of interest in UK HE, with 89% of respondents to the SCONUL Shared Services Survey stating that they were open to 'any arrangement that delivers benefits', and a significant number supported a governance mechanism operated by 'a sector agency' in the style of JANET (UK)' (Kay, 2009). In 2011, JISC Collections was appointed by HEFCE and JISC to take this project forward as Knowledge Base Plus (KB+) (JISC Collections, 2011). The KB+ project aims to develop a central, shared, above-campus knowledge base of electronic resources management data for the UK HE community.

Next-generation library management systems (LMS)

2012 will be a watershed year in the roll out of a new generation of library automation platforms, especially in the academic library arena.

(Breeding, 2012, 1)

Ken Chad has warned that the library management system (LMS) marketplace is 'ripe for disruption' (Chad, 2009) and that the legacy LMS currently in place in most of the UK is beginning to hinder the library by requiring specialist staff knowledge offering fixed workflows leading to duplication of effort, such as rekeying financial information into several systems.

Huddersfield, collaborating with KB+, has been awarded funding by JISC to investigate and evaluate the possibility of integrating data flows between KB+ and local knowledge bases at Huddersfield and the Serials Solutions® knowledge base behind Intota. Intota is a radically new system with little of the legacy baggage associated with traditional LMS (Serials Solutions®, 2012b). The Huddersfield, Intota, KnowledgeBase+ Evaluation (HIKE) project, reporting in early 2013, will look at the potential for collaboration between the systems and evaluate the suitability and potential of Intota as a replacement for the traditional LMS in the UK market and the potential effects of cultural change that such a collaboration would create.

Conclusions

Keep your feet on the ground and keep reaching for the stars.

(Kasem, n.d., cited in Wikipedia, 2012)

Many of the projects discussed in this chapter could not have been developed without the support of JISC or internal university funding. CLS uses JISC calls for funding to enhance services and foster ideas that are at an embryonic stage of development. New ways of funding, such as the JISC Elevator pilot, a crowdsourcing platform encouraging ideas to be submitted in order for the community to vote to show their support of the idea (JISC, 2012), is an ideal way to encourage collaboration and to help small-scale projects flourish.

Although this chapter has been about the use of technology, it is the underlying culture in our libraries that supports the themes discussed. There is a strong culture of collaboration and innovation within CLS, and as a result, staff within the service are encouraged by senior management to attend conferences and internal events and to cultivate ideas. Even in times of fiscal constraint, it is these ideas that have helped to keep Huddersfield moving forward.

Ultimately, the *raison d'être* for the collaborative projects described in this chapter is simple: to show how library services can add value to enrich the student experience and increase attainment. Technology can be used to achieve this, whether it be through simplifying services, by introducing new discovery services and systems, or by sharing data to understand the needs and behaviour of students. The impact of collaboration has been a source of inspiration both to staff at Huddersfield and to others through the various JISC-funded projects and community shared services discussed above. It is hoped that this close collaboration with partners at local, national and international levels will continue and that outputs will result in further lessons being learned by the HE community as a whole.

References

Anderson, P. (2007) *What is Web 2.0? Ideas, technologies and implications for education*, JISC Technology and Standards Watch,
www.jisc.ac.uk/publications/reports/2007/twweb2.aspx.

Anon (2011) *Vlsresearch*, http://vlsresearch.wordpress.com.

Association of College and Research Libraries (ACRL) (2010) *Value of Academic Libraries: a comprehensive research review and report*, researched by Megan Oakleaf, Association of College and Research Libraries,
www.ala.org/ala/mgrps/divs/acrl/issues/value/val_report.pdf.

Balman, L. (2009) Mash Oop North, *CILIP Update*, September, 17,
eprints.hud.ac.uk/5881.

Barrett, L., Evans, J., Harrison, R., Heathcote, D., Jones, L., Osborne, A., Pattern, D., Stone, G. and Thompson, K. (2009) Getting to Know Web 2.0 Tools, *CILIP Update*, November, 40–3, eprints.hud.ac.uk/6524.

Barrett, L., Heathcote, D., Osborne, A., Pattern, D. and Stone, G. (2008) *25 Things @ Huddersfield*, http://eprints.hud.ac.uk/5927.

Bloomsbury Qatar Foundation Journals (2011) Open Access, BQFJ White Paper,

Bloomsbury Qatar Foundation Journals,
www.qscience.com/userimages/ContentEditor/1322148977938/oa-whitepaper.pdf.

Blowers, H. (2006a) *Learning 2.0,* http://plcmcl2-about.blogspot.com.

Blowers, H. (2006b) Hblowers learning2.0Libraries Del.icio.us links,
http://del.icio.us/hblowers/learning2.0Libraries.

Breeding, M. (2012) Smarter Libraries through Technology: what's in store for 2012,
Smart Libraries Newsletter, **XXXII** (1), 1-2,
http://alatechsource.metapress.com/content/u27j7hh85310/?p=aa005fadb22245bd
9df8d9f3e5a814b2&pi=5.

Brook, J., Weaver, M., Pattern, D. and Anderson, S. (2002) The INHALE Project
(Information for Nursing and Health in a Learning Environment): the first year,
VINE, **32** (1), 24-34, doi: 10.1108/03055720210804445.

Chad, K. (2009) *Disrupting libraries,* Charleston Conference, 4-7 November, Charleston,
SC.

Collins, E. (2013) Social Media and Scholarly Communications: the more they change,
the more they stay the same? In Shorley, D. and Jubb, M. (eds), *The Future of
Scholarly Communication,* Facet Publishing, to be published.

Collins, E., Pattern, D. and Stone, G. (2011) *25 Research Things,*
http://25researchthings2011.wordpress.com.

Copac (2012) *Copac Activity Data Project,* http://copac.ac.uk/innovations/activity-data.

Directory of Open Access Journals (2012) *Directory of Open Access Journals,*
www.doaj.org.

EPrints (n.d.) *EPrints Bazaar,* http://bazaar.eprints.org.

Ex Libris (2011) *bX Recommender Service: overview,*
www.exlibrisgroup.com/category/bXOverview.

Gibson, I., Goddard, L. and Gordon, S. (2009) One Box to Search Them All:
implementing federated search at an academic library, *Library Hi Tech,* **27** (1), 118-
33, doi: 10.1108/07378830910942973.

Goodall, D. and Pattern, D. (2011) Academic Library Non/Low Use and Undergraduate
Student Achievement: a preliminary report of research in progress, *Library
Management,* **32** (3), 159-70. doi: 10.1108/01435121111112871.

Imperial College (2011) *Blogs, Twitter, Wikis and Other Web-Based Tools,*
http://research20atimperial.wordpress.com.

JISC (2007) *Social Networking Extensions for EPrints (SNEEP),*
www.jisc.ac.uk/whatwedo/programmes/reppres/sue/sneep.aspx.

JISC (2008) *Towards Implementation of Library 2.0 and the e-Framework (TILE),*
www.jisc.ac.uk/whatwedo/programmes/resourcediscovery/tile.aspx.

JISC (2011) *JISC Activity Data,*
www.jisc.ac.uk/whatwedo/programmes/inf11/activitydata.aspx.

JISC (2012) *JISC Elevator,* http://elevator.jisc.ac.uk.

JISC Collections (2011) *Knowledge Base+*, www.jisc-collections.ac.uk/knowledgebaseplus/.

Kasem, C. (2012) *Casey Kasem*, http://en.wikipedia.org/wiki/Casey_Kasem.

Kay, D. (2009) *SCONUL Shared Services*, http://sconulss.blogspot.co.uk.

KPMG (2006) *Shared Services in the Higher Education Sector*, report to HEFCE by KPMG and HEFCE, http://webarchive.nationalarchives.gov.uk/20100202100434/http://www.hefce.ac.uk/pubs/rdreports/2006//rd15_06/rd15_06.pdf.

Lister, P. (2007) One Desk + One Stop = One Solution. In *ALIA National Library and Information Technicians Conference Papers*, www.alia.org.au/conferences/nlitc.2007.papers/one.desk.pdf.

McMaster University (2007) *Learning 2.0 @ Mac*, http://macetg.wordpress.com/about-learning-20-mac.

Margie H. J. and Cox, B. (2010) Measuring the Value of Library Resources and Student Academic Performance through Relational Datasets. In *Proceedings of the Library Assessment Conference: building effective, sustainable, practical assessment*, http://ro.uow.edu.au/cgi/viewcontent.cgi?article=1120&context=asdpapers.

Murdoch University (2007) *Murdoch University Library 23 Things*, http://mullet23.blogspot.co.uk.

Newman, B. (2011) *Librarian by Day*, http://librarianbyday.net.

Nicholas, D. (2008) If We Do Not Understand Our Users, We Will Certainly Fail. In Stone, G., Anderson, R. and Feinstein, J. (eds), *E-Resources Management Handbook*, UK Serials Group, doi: 10.1629/9552448_0_3.13.1.

Open Data Commons (n.d.) *Open Data Commons: legal tools for open data*, www.opendatacommons.org.

O'Reilly, T. (2006) *Web 2.0 Compact Definition: trying again*, http://radar.oreilly.com/2006/12/web-20-compact-definition-tryi.html.

Pattern, D. (2008) *Free Book Usage Data from the University of Huddersfield*, www.daveyp.com/blog/archives/528.

Pattern, D. (2009) *OPAC 2.0 and Beyond*, 32nd UKSG Annual Conference and Exhibition, eprints.hud.ac.uk/4143.

Pattern, D. (2011a) *My Reading Project*, http://library.hud.ac.uk/blogs/projects/myreading.

Pattern, D. (2011b) *Library Impact Data Project Data*, eprints.hud.ac.uk/11543.

Pattern, D., Thoburn, J., Coates, A. and Stone, G. (2010) *Summon4hn*, http://library.hud.ac.uk/blogs/projects/summon4hn.

RCUK (2012) *RCUK Proposed Policy on Access to Research Outputs*, Research Councils UK, www.openscholarship.org/upload/docs/application/pdf/2012-03/rcuk_proposed_policy_on_access_to_research_outputs.pdf.

RIN (2010) *If You Build It, Will They Come? How researchers perceive and use Web 2.0*,

Research Information Network,
www.rin.ac.uk/our-work/communicating-and-disseminating-research/
use-and-relevance-web-20-researchers.

Running in the Halls (2011) *Lemon Tree*,
www.hud.ac.uk/tali/projects/tl_projects_11/lemon_tree/.

Serials Solutions® (n.d.) *Summon Community Wiki*,
http://community.summon.serials solutions.com/index.php/Main_Page.

Serials Solutions® (2012a) *360 Search XML API*,
www.serials solutions.com/en/services/360-search/xml-api.

Serials Solutions® (2012b) *Intota*, www.serials solutions.com/en/services/intota.

Serials Solutions® User Group UK (n.d.) User Group, blog,
http://ssuguk.wordpress.com.

Sero (2009) *JISC MOSAIC*, www.sero.co.uk/jisc-mosaic.html.

Sharman, A. (2011) *Roving Librarian Proposal to the Teaching and Learning Institute*,
unpublished.

Society for College, National and University Libraries (SCONUL) (2010) SCONUL
Shared Services Seminar, 22 November, Institute of Mechanical Engineers,
www.sconul.ac.uk/sharedservices/seminar_nov2010.

Stone, G. (2009) Resource Discovery. In Woodward, H. and Estelle, L. (eds), *Digital
Information: order or anarchy?*, Facet Publishing, 133–63.

Stone, G. (2010) Searching Life, the Universe and Everything? The implementation of
Summon at the University of Huddersfield, *LIBER Quarterly*, **20** (1), 25–51,
http://liber.library.uu.nl/index.php/lq/article/view/7974/8278.

Stone, G. (2011) *Huddersfield Open Access Publishing (HOAP) Toolkit*,
eprints.hud.ac.uk/12239.

Stone, G., Collins, E. and Pattern, D. (2012) Digging Deeper into Library Data:
understanding how library usage and other factors affect student outcomes. In
LIBER 41st Annual Conference, eprints.hud.ac.uk/12973.

Stone, G., Pattern, D. and Ramsden, B. (2011a) Does Library Use Affect Student
Attainment? A preliminary report on the Library Impact Data Project, *LIBER
Quarterly*, **21** (1), 5–22,
http://liber.library.uu.nl/index.php/lq/article/view/8005.

Stone, G., Pattern, D. and Ramsden, B. (2011b) The Library Impact Data Project: hit miss
or maybe. In *9th Northumbria International Conference on Performance Measurement in
Libraries and Information Services: proving value in challenging times*, University of
York, eprints.hud.ac.uk/10210.

Stone, G., Ramsden, B. and Pattern, D. (2011a) *Library Impact Data Project*,
http://library.hud.ac.uk/blogs/projects/lidp.

Stone, G., Ramsden, B. and Pattern, D. (2011b) *LIDP Toolkit*, eprints.hud.ac.uk/11571.

Stone, G., Ramsden, B. and Pattern, D. (2011c) Looking for the Link between Library

Usage and Student Attainment, *Ariadne,* **67**, www.ariadne.ac.uk/issue67/stone-et-al.

Stone, G., White, S., Robinson, D., Pitchford, I. and Edmunds, C. (2012) *Huddersfield Open Access Publishing Final Report, project report,* University of Huddersfield, eprints.hud.ac.uk/13278.

Tenopir, C. (2009) Visualize the Perfect Search, *Library Journal,* March, www.libraryjournal.com/article/CA6639354.html?industryid=47130.

Thoburn, J., Coates, A. and Stone, G. (2010) *Simplifying Resource Discovery and Access in Academic Libraries: implementing and evaluating Summon at Huddersfield and Northumbria Universities, project report,* Northumbria University and University of Huddersfield, eprints.hud.ac.uk/9921.

Thoburn, J. Coates, A. and Stone, G. (2012) Simplifying Resource Discovery and Access in Academic Libraries: implementing and evaluating Summon at Huddersfield and Northumbria Universities. In Popp, M. P. and Dallis, D. (eds), *Planning and Implementing Resource Discovery Tools in Academic Libraries,* IGI Global.

University of Glasgow (2004) *JeLit, a Journal of E-Literacy,* www.jelit.org.

University of Huddersfield (n.d.) *Teaching and Learning Institute,* www2.hud.ac.uk/tali.

University of Huddersfield (2009) *Teaching in Lifelong Learning,* eprints.hud.ac.uk/journal_till.

University of Huddersfield (2012) *University of Huddersfield Repository,* eprints.hud.ac.uk.

Walsh, J. and Pollack, R. (2007) *Open Knowledge 1.0: March 17 2007,* http:/en.wikiquote.org/wiki/Free_software..

White, S. and Stone, G. (2010a) Maximising Use of Library Resources at the University of Huddersfield, *Serials,* **23** (2), 83-90, doi: 10.1629/2383.

White, S. and Stone, G. (2010b) Maximising Use of Library Resources at the University of Huddersfield. In: *UKSG 33rd Annual Conference and Exhibition, 12-14 April 2010, Edinburgh International Conference Centre,* eprints.hud.ac.uk/7248.

Whitton, N. and Jones, R. (2009) Alternate Reality Gaming to Support Information Literacy, *ALISS Quarterly,* **4** (4), 18-21.

Willetts, D. (2012a) *Public Access to Publicly-Funded Research,* www.bis.gov.uk/news/speeches/david-willetts-public-access-to-research.

Willetts, D (2012b) Open, Free Access to Academic Research? This will be a seismic shift, *Guardian,* 1 May, www.guardian.co.uk/commentisfree/2012/may/01/open-free-access-academic-research.

8 Space: changing the boundaries

Liz Jolly, Teesside University, UK

Introduction

This chapter considers developments in collaborative approaches to the enhancement of academic library space.

Brophy defined the purpose of the academic library as follows:

> Academic libraries are here to enable and enhance learning in all its forms –
> whether it be the learning of a first year undergraduate coming to terms with what
> is meant by higher education or the learning of a Nobel Prize winning scientist
> seeking to push forwards the frontiers of her discipline.
>
> (Brophy, 2005, 216)

First, these developments are viewed in the context of changes in higher education, learning and teaching and technology. The second section considers examples of collaborative approaches and the final section of the chapter attempts to evaluate these developments in terms of learning enhancement, rather than of space efficiency. While it is crucial to integrate physical and virtual learning spaces, this chapter will focus on physical library spaces.

Context

Developments in learning space design methodologies are driven by and impacted upon by changes in the higher education sector, by approaches to learning and teaching and by developments in technology, and these are considered briefly here.

Higher education, learning and teaching

A key element of institutional policies in the UK and elsewhere has been the emphasis on active learning and the development of students as independent lifelong learners. More recently this has been supplemented by issues such as personalization and ownership of learning as outlined in *Higher Education in a Web 2.0 World* (Committee of Inquiry into the Changing Learner Experience, CLEX, 2009).

In the UK 'enhancing the student experience' is a key focus of funding councils, the Quality Assurance Agency and the Higher Education Academy, as mentioned in Chapter 5. The Ramsden report (2008) highlighted the importance of students as partners in developing their own learning experience, which is a 'joint responsibility' between them and their institution. In many universities students are now involved in formal and informal decision-making and planning.

Changes in the higher education sector, including the expansion of a fees culture (Department for Business, Innovation and Skills, 2011) and the National Student Survey and other surveys, have resulted in differentiation in the marketplace. Universities will have to be clear about their complete offer to students as they try to attract fee-paying students as customers and to manage the different perception held by students of themselves as learners and as consumers/customers.

Therefore institutions need to take a holistic view of learning and the student experience. The development of collaborative approaches across institutions has reflected this in the UK both in terms of 'super-convergence' of university services such as libraries, student services and registry (see Chapter 9) and in terms of joint initiatives, such as 'one-stop-shop' approaches to information points for students, even where such services remain organizationally separate. In the USA the paper *Learning Reconsidered* (Keeling, 2004) articulates that the student learning experience is not merely classroom-based and involves cross-institutional collaboration.

Current higher education learning and teaching practice reflects post-industrial society with changes in pedagogy and a shift towards constructivist models in a post-industrialist age. Light and Cox (2001, 18) note that this is almost a 'secular religion' in the sector, and while theorists differ on whether they stress the importance of biological and cognitive mechanisms (Piaget) or social factors (Vygotsky, Lave) there is general agreement that knowledge is constructed by learners based upon their current/past knowledge and experiences and has resulted in the incorporation of collaborative approaches to learning in curriculum delivery.

Technology

From their research in Canada, Doiron and Asselin (2011, 230) note that 'In many cases we seem to have been tinkering [with technologies] to make them fit into the traditions and values long held for tertiary education. This will not get us to where we need to be if we are to be relevant and robust learning communities.' In the UK the Committee of Inquiry into the Changing Learner Experience (CLEX) was convened in acknowledgement of the critical impact of technology on higher education. Its aim was to enquire into 'the strategic and policy implications for higher education of the changing experience and expectations of learners in the light of their increasing use of the newest technologies'. It noted that the current generation of students are managing a disjuncture between their world and that of higher education – and that future generations will not be so accommodating (CLEX, 2009, 5, 7).

In the USA, Oblinger and Oblinger (2005, 2.9–2.10) identify this generation as the 'Net Generation' (also called 'Millennials' by Rowlands and Nicolas [2008] and 'Digital Natives' by Prensky [2001]) and for them 'the Internet is like oxygen; they can't imagine being able to live without it. . . . What we might consider new technology such as blogs or wikis are not thought of as technology by students.' However, the Net Generation are not satisfied with web-only courses; they have certain expectations about higher education in addition to their desire to be connected with people and to be social. It is the way that they do this that is different. But students still come to college to meet people, to socialize and to engage with faculty. Oblinger and Oblinger recommend that institutions engage in dialogue with learners before investing in technology or buildings rather than relying on past assumptions.

McLaughlin and Mills (2008, 3) list the key changes in learning and teaching in Australian universities over the past two decades in terms of technology, learning models, communities of learning, professional learning, third-space learning and non-sequential learning. They note that developing learning spaces to enable these trends is paramount to the future of institutions. The next section considers how these contextual developments have influenced library space design and the emergence of collaborative approaches.

Libraries and space development

Given the above complexity, library services and spaces need to be more closely aligned with mission and strategic priorities of their institutions. Library space planning is becoming, and needs to continue to become, an institution-wide collaborative activity.

Although for a time it seemed that technology would negate the need for on-campus library services, in the past 20 years or so there has been a sea change in thinking about university libraries as learning spaces together with the acceptance that PCs could be more than tools for individual learning. The widespread adoption of technology to enable and support learning would need new types of spaces for learning. Indeed as Freeman (2005, 2) and others argued, technology has actually become the catalyst that 'transforms the library into a more vital and critical intellectual centre of life at colleges and universities'. The UK Joint Information Systems Committee (JISC) project Designing Spaces for Effective Learning (JISC, 2006) looked at how learning and teaching spaces across institutions, including libraries, should develop to enable technology enhanced learning effectively. One of its key findings was that for success an integrated approach was necessary, including the involvement of collaborative teams (estates/facilities, library and ICT senior managers) in development projects. These also need to include a shared understanding of vision and goals between architects and institutions (JISC, 2006, 13).

Hunter, Lidgy and Robert (2005) further analysed the work of this project and found that there were two key drivers required for the effective development and implementation of new types of learning spaces. Operational drivers originated in factors affecting organizational effectiveness while pedagogic drivers affected the learning and teaching experience of students and arose from institutional strategies and course delivery methods. Without both these drivers present projects were unlikely to be successful. And without pedagogy as the main driver 'institutions may simply replace like with like' (Hunter, Lidgy and Robert, 5). They reiterate the importance of collaborative approaches to space development involving academic and professional support services staff from across the institution. According to their study, students were not then seen as having any direct input into the management or development of learning spaces in top-level committees by institutions consulted, but Hunter, Lidgy and Robert note that they are key to the development process.

Today there is an acknowledgement of the importance of putting the learner at the centre of what we do. Libraries are moving from being collection-centred to being student-centred; away from being, as Freeman (2005, 1) notes, 'first and foremost as places to collect, access and preserve print collections' and away from having a large amount of space devoted to library operations. Initial changes to the degree of access and space given to collections were driven by changes in technology. Now there are moves towards using technology as an enabler with a focus on learning. This shift has also been enabled by developments in collections management (such as shelf-ready book supply and electronic resources provision), which enable library space to be freed up (see, for example, Lewis on page 139).

Collaborative design of library and learning spaces

If we put the learner at the centre of our developments, then as Malcolm Brown (2005) has argued, learning theory should inform all other decisions about learning space design within our institutions and a vision for learning spaces should be underpinned by this. Design of spaces should also include students.

> Learning space design requires a collaborative, integrated approach with an overarching vision that informs and support specific projects.
>
> (Brown, 2005, 2.2)

Eigenbrodt (2008, 14) believes that Hannah Arendt's model of the public sphere can be adapted to the development of academic libraries. Societal space will enable people to come together to develop: places which can bring people together, spaces 'which allow users to discover and configure the space for themselves' without preventing seclusion in quieter areas.

Gayton (2008, 64, 60) attempts to clarify the difference between communal and social learning and issue in design. He argues that communal activity in academic libraries is 'a solitary activity; it is studious contemplative, and quiet' as opposed to 'social activity which is group activity . . . it is certainly not quiet'. Gayton quotes Ranseen (2002) who had already noted that 'communal study in a library fosters a silent exchange of energy and quiet study is in truth an active experience'. Gayton further argues that social learning spaces should not undermine the 'fundamentally communal character' of the academic library.

What these ideas illustrate is the importance of retaining traditional aspects of library spaces and for these not becoming an afterthought in design. The relationship between library and learning environments, collaborative practice and the resulting configuration of space is next explored, with notable examples.

Library design continuum

It is important that we view library space within our institutions as a continuum from completely silent to completely social and that we offer a range of spaces on this continuum for our communities to suit different individuals and also the same individual at different times – it may well be that the same person who is the life and soul of the social areas at the beginning of the academic year is the mainstay of the silent areas at the end. In its 2012 refurbishment, for example, Teesside University in the UK is combining the introduction of social learning spaces with the creation, for the first time, of a discrete silent study area by partitioning off a formerly open atrium on one floor. Sunderland University has the Catherine Cookson Reading Room, a silent space (University of Sunderland, n.d.), and the Information Commons at Sheffield University has a silent study area as part of its provision of a variety of spaces. Both these spaces certainly encourage communal learning and would also seem to embody Frischer's (2005, 50) 'drama of community'.

I would argue that we should adapt our traditional model of library services of 'space, resources and staff (who deliver services and support)' to one of 'space, technology (including access and resources) and pedagogy'. This would fully reflect institutional priorities and enable the library and information profession in higher education to embed its service and space development within the broader context of developments within the sector.

The library as a facilitator of learning

Nitecki (2011, 31) states library space still has three main functions, whether these are the core mission or merely coexisting roles:

- accumulator (resources and equipment)
- service provider (interrogation retrieval, circulation of materials and customer support)
- facilitator (through the design of environments for autonomous learning and knowledge creation).

Many would argue that it is the facilitation role which is key for the future of physical library space, and the work of Kathlin Ray (2002, cited by Nitecki) would seem to bear this out. Ray's paradigms emphasize the change of library accentuated values over time: resources or holdings (before 1980), access (1980), use by students (1995) and learning transformation (predicted for 2010).

Library services: contemplative and collaborative

The Education Advisory Board of the (US) University Leadership Council (2011, 63) has surveyed university librarians to find the 'top trends in next generation library space planning'. These are:

- fewer physical resources
- comfort and collaboration
- flexibility and modularity
- wireless connectivity and outlet access
- integration of academic support services and food and drink.

These would seem to mirror planning considerations already in operation, which reflect broader changes in the higher education landscape. Libraries have had to develop spaces to support a broader range of learning activities and styles, course delivery modes and attendance patterns.

The first example of this, and for many still the most radical interpretation in the UK, is the Saltire Centre at Glasgow Caledonian University. Much has been written of this development, which attempts to put the building at the centre of the campus and the learner at the centre of the development in creating a campus learning hub. The building was the result of cross-institutional collaboration between students, library, student services and estates professionals, as well as learning and teaching specialists in the design period. The operation and delivery of services reflect an ongoing partnership between these services and students. The Principal viewed the Saltire Centre as 'an overt strategy to re-socialize the University and encourage conversation between students and staff that engage the whole community as co-learners, exposing their understanding and ideas to those of others. It is this questioning and dialogue that lead to deep understanding of concepts and ideas' (JISC Infonet, n.d.).

Integrated learning environments

The information commons movement was particularly significant in its attempt to integrate library and learning provision with the broader student learning experience independent of organizational structure. Early adopters included the University of Calgary, the University of Auckland, the University of Iowa and the University of Southern California. As the emphasis on learning underpinned by technology, rather than technology as an end in itself, has regained ground, this has been reflected in the names of these developments with 'learning commons' gaining in popularity.

Beagle (2010, 14) notes how the physical spaces in an information or learning commons are an expression of a learning support-focused approach. He cites research by Nagata (2009) of the link between the information or learning commons and the Japanese concept of Ba: 'shared space for emerging relationships'. The space can be physical, virtual, mental or any combination of them but is concerned with the concept of knowledge creation.

Increasingly the term 'learning commons' has been used to differentiate spaces where a number of university services (in addition to library and IT departments) have come together to support students in a more collaborative and holistic way, as reflected in the importance of student success and employability. These services may include academic writing, media and so on, but also curriculum development. The library has been developed as 'an integrated learning environment' (University of Auckland, n.d.) that 'fosters informal, collaborative and creative work, and social interaction' (University of Massachusetts Amherst, n.d.).

In the UK the 'commons' name has most notably been taken up by two institutions from the Russell Group of research-led institutions. The University of Sheffield has integrated its undergraduate library into its Information Commons. Development of this space and support within it has involved collaboration between the University Library and University IT services, two operationally distinct services with a single manager, as well as with the School of Information Sciences, which manages the Centre for Inquiry-Based Learning in the Arts and Social Sciences (CILASS) space within the building (University of Sheffield, n.d.). The University of Manchester has developed a Learning Commons that, while managed by the University of Manchester Library, is in a separate building and aims to provide 'a world-class 21st century learning environment' (University of Manchester, n.d.). It opened in September 2012.

As Bennett (2006, 11) noted, 'a library fit for purpose cannot be designed around self-referential service concerns as libraries customarily are today'. For libraries that are 'something more than traditional dressed as new' we must 'relax the dominance of traditional services in library planning, focus on the learning behaviours of readers and self-consciously use space to enable community based learning'. Bennett advocates embracing the virtual library as part of this new approach. Only the situating of information in the social context of learning can justify the immense investments made in new library space.

The content of some of these initiatives does not differ very much from what is already on offer in many academic libraries in the UK. However, the importance of the cultural concept of the library being at the heart of the learning process is evident. This enables us to reclaim the idea of the university as a community of learners with the library at its heart and presents significant opportunities for academic libraries within their institutions.

Student collaboration

The acknowledgement that the student experience is broader than just what happens in the lecture theatre and how this impacts on the library has further helped to focus institutions on the importance of libraries. This has been accompanied in the UK by the emergence of student engagement and the student voice as key issues in higher education, and of the collaborative development of facilities and services as an important element of this (see, e.g., Corbyn, 2012).

It is now usual (in the UK at least) for students to be members of space design and refurbishment project boards within universities or, as a minimum, to have been consulted via focus groups or as advisors. In contrast at Fresno State

University students have played a key role in the design of the refurbished University Library via ethnographic studies (as detailed below), and Twait (2009) has written about her experience of offering a course in theoretical design of a library as a third place.

The development of the new library at Macquarie University (Brodie, 2008) also involved developing strategies for student involvement in the design of learning spaces. Additional collaboration took place with some of the University's school partners as some final year students would become university undergraduates in the following academic year.

Leadership

Library services are increasingly seen as leaders in developing and managing learning spaces outside the library building. The following UK case studies demonstrate the extended and influential role of the library where space initiatives have enabled academic libraries to lead collaborative projects on behalf of their institutions.

The Learning Gateway at the University of Cumbria in the UK aims to be 'the home of flexible learning' on the Carlisle campus. 'It is an innovative, interactive and adaptable space that offers students, visitors and staff an exciting and diverse range of learning opportunities and experiences. It has embedded technology and wireless network throughout' (University of Cumbria, n.d.). The space is managed by Learning, Information and Student Services, the department including the library and student services. The space houses the Centre for the Development and Enhancement of Professional Practice in order to provide critical underpinning of the University's Learning and Teaching Strategy with the aim of supporting teaching-staff development.

Teesside University Library and Information Services manages 'The Corner', a postgraduate learning space in the student union building catering for those who want a more informal but still serious study space.

Bradford University's Student Central is intended to offer social learning spaces, career-oriented activities, self-development and curriculum activities. The space includes social learning areas and a café, seminar rooms and a tiered lecture theatre with a 'learning mall' connecting with the library. The vision for the space was that it would 'work in synergy with the J. B. Priestley [University] Library as one learning environment', creating a 'fusion of space' (University of Bradford, 2011).

The University of Bolton's library has been part of a learning mall of student-focused services. Refurbished in 2011 as the Chancellor's Mall this now includes the Social Learning Zone: 'a more chilled out version of a library' (University of Bolton, n.d.).

Exeter University's refurbished library is in the context of the development of a learning forum, which aims to provide 'an inspirational range of learning facilities'. These include a new Student Services Centre, technology-rich learning spaces, a 400-seat auditorium, retail and catering outlets and the University reception. The building opened in May 2012. The University's registrar David Allen stated: 'What is absolutely essential is that it works for the students. It needs to be flexible so that if future needs change the buildings can be easily adjusted to suit, and flexible so that spaces can potentially be used for a range of activity' (University of Exeter, n.d.).

Portsmouth's 'Third Space' aims to be students' 'home from home' on campus. It was inspired by elements of the Saltire Centre, mentioned previously. It offers social learning spaces and access to student union facilities in an alcohol-free environment. It is part of a clear University strategy to offer a variety of learning spaces on campus, including traditional library space and library open access computing, as well as facilities for 'student led' activities (University of Portsmouth, n.d.).

Within the library space envelope De Montfort University has developed the Learning Zone in partnership with the Centre for Learning and Study Support, which is now organizationally within the same department as the library. Towlson and Pillai (2008, 25) note the importance of the library as a hub of independent learning and believe that the co-location of library IT and student support services has led to an increase in student use of available support services.

Teesside University Library has for many years managed the University's Drop-in Student Skills Centre which is housed within the University library building. The service was reviewed in 2011 and as a consequence of the review and of the partial refurbishment of the library, the new Learning Hub will be a core element of the University's work on integrating independent learning and skills development. The project will connect 'spokes' in the University's academic schools with other support services and with the Students' Union.

An institutional view of library learning spaces

The institutional development of learning spaces and their impact on students' learning development was an aim of the (UK) Learn Higher Centre for Excellence in Teaching and Learning (CETL) (Learn Higher CETL, 2010). The CETL, a consortium of ten institutions from different mission groups, had the intention of enabling diverse learners to achieve their maximum potential. As part of the project, libraries at Liverpool University and Kent Medway campus developed new learning spaces.

Research undertaken at Bradford University as part of the Higher Education

Retention and Engagement Project (Lefebre amd Bashir, 2011) found that various aspects of the student experience influenced the retention and engagement of students. Of these 'belonging' was associated with belonging not only to other people and the course and department but also to the wider campus and university, and the importance of spaces, both physical and virtual was emphasized. The project examined the issue of belonging in relation to physical space on campus via open-ended survey responses and interviews. Flexibility of space correlated with popularity: 'The most popular places, however, emerged were those which offered multiple resources or usage – so spaces where they could meet friends, socialize and eat, but also study and do group work' (2011, 4). These multiple-use spaces were important, as were places designated for quiet study and privacy or relaxation.

Is the natural end of these collaborations the end of library space? David Lewis, in his article 'A Strategy for Library Services in the First Quarter of the 21st Century' (Lewis, 2007), suggests that the natural consequences of digitization of existing stock and purchase of new electronic resources is that space will be made available for learning. However, 'Library space will need to be shared with a variety of partners, and it is likely that the distinction between the library and other informal campus space will blur.' He argues for 'campus conversations' to determine future form and function of library space and that giving space back to the institution will be a natural consequence of this (2007, 423).

Keating and Gabb's 'principles of learning commons' (2005) reflect both the move from service to learner as noted by Bennett (2006) and also a move to a broader, institution-wide strategic approach based on collaboration and responsiveness to changing needs. A further development of this approach has been demonstrated in the collaborative design implemented at California Polytechnic State University and further developed by San José State University (written about elsewhere in this volume). Somerville and Collins (2008) write about the application of this approach at both institutions and how the elements – a process (user-centric, interdisciplinary continuous investigations), an outcome (usable products), applications, environments and a philosophy (learning focus and relationship building) – develop an inherent learning orientation to space and service development.

Collaboration with faculty

While new technology enabled learning spaces may improve student *satisfaction* with facilities at their institution, Lippincott (2009) notes that the integration of spaces, technology and curriculum is key to improvements in student learning. However, this is unlikely to happen without the engagement of teaching staff from the beginning of any such project. In specialized spaces the learning requirements of the disciplines need to drive the planning process. Lippincott quotes the Project Kaleidoscope organization in the USA, which has created resources for space planning and engagement with academic staff. Central to this is the opportunity afforded by linking space to 'insights about how people learn, which needs then to translate into curricular reform . . . illustrat[ing] the inter-relationship between curriculum, spaces and goals for student learning' (2009, 18). Lippincott (2006) cites learning and information commons as success stories of collaboration between academic and support departments. This can be true whether the facilities have been developed as an integral part of the library building or are separate to the university library building even when 'owned' by the library department.

The JISC Learning Landscapes in Higher Education project (Neary et al., 2010) looked at collaborative developments in learning spaces across a several institutions from different mission groups. The project aimed to 'make a very clear connection between research into effective teaching and the design of learning spaces, as well as demonstrating how to establish a relationship between design and pedagogical theory' (2010, 11). Findings included that the engagement of students and staff (academic and support), pedagogy as a design principle and alignment of design with institutional priorities were all key elements of successful landscape design.

The issue of staff learning and development in relation to enabling effective learning in new kinds of spaces was mentioned by Lippincott (2009) and Wilson and Randall (2012) and is the focus of current JISC projects regarding digital literacies (JISC, n.d.). It is obviously pertinent to academic staff delivering learning and is also a key consideration in the learning facilitation and support offered by library staff in library spaces.

The final section of this chapter reviews attempts to evaluate the effectiveness of libraries as learning spaces and their contribution to students' learning.

The effectiveness of libraries as learning spaces

So how do we assess whether these developments have enhanced students' experience and contributed to improving their learning?

The UK Higher Education Space Management Group reviewed the impact of developments in spaces in the UK sector in terms of more efficient space utilization (UKSMG, 2006). However, it is important for evaluation not to focus solely on this aspect.

While the higher education sector in the UK as a whole, as mentioned elsewhere, is moving towards a more student-centred focus, Bligh and Pearshouse (2011) at the University of Nottingham noted that evaluation of learning spaces in general still comes from a perspective of spatial determinism and a focus on the space rather than the learning. Evaluation needs to acknowledge learning as a cognitive experience.

The JISC Study of Effective Evaluation Models and Practices for Technology Supported Physical Learning Spaces (JELS) aimed to identify and review the tools, methods and frameworks used to evaluate technology supported or enhanced physical learning spaces (Pearshouse et al., 2009). The final report identified a need for the higher education sector 'to reconsider how to evaluate physical learning spaces, so as to assess more clearly how they satisfy design intentions and teaching and learning needs' (2009, 4) and proposed a conceptual Framework for Evaluating Learning Spaces (FELS).

In the USA there is evidence of further development of evaluation methodologies. Dayton University has been concerned with developing an institution-wide approach to the assessment of learning and teaching spaces. A multi-year study was commenced in 2004 with a rationale based on links between spaces, pedagogy and the academic programme. In the middle of the project it emerged that student engagement was the best measure for learning as assessing specific learning outcomes was too complex. Hunley and Schaller (2009, 6) note in this context that 'without assessment, institutions may miss the important connections between context, institutional culture and students' specific needs'.

Radcliffe (2008) has developed the Pedagogy-Space-Technology (PST) Design and Evaluation Framework. Key questions for evaluating learning spaces are framed within each of these areas. Wilson and Randall (2012) have used this methodology to evaluate 'next generation learning spaces' at Bond University in Australia. These spaces were influenced by the Australian Learning and Teaching Council's Next Generation Learning Spaces Project. They used observation, focused interviews and surveys of staff and students and concluded that further investigation is needed in areas of learner interactivity, learner engagement, use of technologies (by both staff and students), impact of furniture and discipline-specific approaches to use of the space.

As a profession we have perhaps been guilty in the past of assuming that we know what is best for our students. Evaluation of the effectiveness of our learning spaces has been an area for development. The JISC Library Impact Data Project (JISC, 2011), discussed in depth in Chapter 7, found that there was no correlation between *visits* to the library and degree class. However, information from recent refurbishments, for example at Northumbria University, suggests that if the space is more relevant to students then they will visit more often and stay for longer.

Roberts and Weaver (2006) argued that rigorous evaluation studies must be underpinned by sound theoretical frameworks in order to understand the complexities of the student experience in blended learning environments.

In the USA the authors of the library study at Fresno State University contended that the design of library services and spaces would benefit from the ethnographic study of its students (Delcore, Mullooly and Scroggins, 2009). The study was informed by ethnographic studies of the student experience at the University of Rochester (Foster and Gibbons, 2007). The Fresno State work is interesting in that the issues facing the university, ethnicity, class and retention as well as off-campus residency, would be recognized by many institutions elsewhere. The need for the library to fit into the broader demands of student life as well as campus life was a key consideration. The study was an example of collaboration from across professional backgrounds and also attempted to 'illuminate the texture, rhythm and experience of university student life in general' (Delcore, Mullooly and Scroggins, 2009, 5).

In the UK, Fraser (2009) analysed the impact of the information commons using a theory-of-change model including ethnographic interviews. The analysis captured students' own explanations for their behaviour, which indicated how far their use of space was influenced by the design of the information commons. Bryant, Matthews and Walton (2009) used ethnographic methodologies at Loughborough University to assess the effectiveness of the new 'Open' space in the main University library. The space was 'designed to provide library users with somewhere they could engage in individual or group activity . . . it is the only area where users can study but are also permitted to chat, eat and drink' (2009, 10). The study was small scale and did not have the aim of linking library use with learner success and learning outcomes. However, it garnered useful findings for incorporation into library service development and was helpful in assessing how far the building has met its design aims and objectives.

One of the Fresno findings relating to space is that future marketing efforts should focus on the diversity of learning spaces. This resonates with findings elsewhere – in the UK, there is a reported swing back to a demand for traditional library spaces from academic library directors in addition to a continuing demand for group and social learning spaces. What current students mean by traditional spaces may well be different from library-staff interpretation and again assumptions about separation from technology in silent spaces may not always be appropriate.

Illinois State University used student-led ethnographic research (Hunter and Ward, 2011) to assess developments in the University's Milner Library. The work started as collaboration between an anthropologist (Hunter) and a librarian (Ward). Ethnography was considered to be an appropriate methodology because students may initially be unaware of how they study or share the same vocabulary as librarians and 'ethnographic methods are useful for capturing the largely unconscious cultural beliefs and practices' (2011, 265). The project tapped into students' native expertise and their easy rapport with peers. One interesting finding was that some students continue to come to the library to find quiet or less distraction. 'Students choose to study in the library because it allows access to all of those services while offering quiet spaces free of distraction' (2011, 267).

An initial assessment of a 'Learning Studio' at the University of Missouri-St Louis has been described by Tom, Voss and Scheetz (2008). One of the drivers for the development of the space is mentioned as competitiveness, as well as the need to meet the requirements of an accrediting body for linking continuous improvement and student learning outcomes. An attempt was made to gather qualitative and quantitative data during one semester and methods used included staff observation of student behaviour, video observations, surveys and staff debriefing meetings. Obviously more flexible use of space, including changes to PC layout and wireless connectivity, will impact on usage density, and Tom, Voss and Scheetz note that 'An institutional debate should address the potentially competing goals of effective learning versus the efficient use of facilities' (2008, 50).

I would argue that the debate is really about what effective use of learning space, including libraries, really means.

Conclusions

Library spaces have transformed in recent years in response to changes in the broader higher education sector, in technological developments and in learning, teaching and learner behaviour. As described in this chapter, the provision of technology-rich environments, integrating the physical and the virtual, and use of flexible spaces are key elements of these developments. The importance of space in the library as an enabler and facilitator in learning cannot be underestimated and it is crucial that librarians play a key role in the debate and ensure that our spaces remain aligned to the institutional mission and be relevant to the student learning experience. Relationships that underpin space design for learning and teaching in the 21st century are increasingly complex and librarians need to work collaboratively with students and with academic and professional services leaders across the changing boundaries of their institutions to develop a full understanding of the impact of new spaces and to articulate clearly and strategically the importance of the library space to the institution.

If the central purpose of the academic library is concerned with learning, as Brophy (2005) stated, then librarians need to ensure that we take a collaborative, holistic and strategic approach to ensure that we deliver the most effective library spaces possible for the benefit of our learning communities:

> It is by realigning libraries with institutional mission that the paradigm for the future will be found.   (Bennett, 2005, 23)

References

Beagle, D. (2010) The Emergent Information Commons: philosophy, models and 21st century learning paradigms, *Journal of Library Administration*, **50**, 7-26.

Bennett, S. (2005) Righting the Balance. In Smith, K. (ed.), *Library as Place: rethinking roles, rethinking space*, Council on Library and Information Resources.

Bennett, S. (2006) The Choice for Learning, *Journal of Academic Librarianship*, **32** (1), 3-13.

Bligh, B. and Pearshouse, I. (2011) Doing Learning Space Evaluations. In Boddington, A. and Boys, J. (eds), *Reshaping Learning: a critical reader: the future of learning spaces in post-compulsory education*, Sense.

Brodie, M. (2008) Watch this Space! Designing a new library for Macquarie University, *The VALA 2008 14th Biennial Conference and Exhibition: libraries/changing spaces, virtual places, 5-7 February 2008, Melbourne*.

Brophy, P. (2005) *The Academic Library*, 2nd edn, Facet Publishing.

Brown, M. (2005) Learning Spaces. In Oblinger, D. G. and Oblinger, J. L. (eds), *Educating the Net Generation*, EDUCAUSE.

Bryant, J., Matthews, G. and Walton, G. (2009) Academic Libraries and Social and Learning Space: a case study of Loughborough University Library, UK, *Journal of Librarianship and Information Science*, **41** (1), 7-18.

Committee of Inquiry into the Changing Learner Experience (CLEX) (2009) *Higher Education in a Web 2.0 World: report of an independent committee of inquiry into the impact on higher education of students' widespread use of Web 2.0 technologies*, Joint Information Systems Committee.

Corbyn, Z. (2012) Dundee Tops THE Student Experience Survey as Fees Put Focus on 'Value for Money', *Times Higher Education*, 26 April, www.timeshighereducation.co.uk/story.asp?storycode=419771.

Delcore, H. D., Mullooly, J. and Scroggins, M. (2009) *The Library Study at Fresno State*, California State University, http://myweb.cwpost.liu.edu/hchu/NJUST2012/Readings/DelcoreEtAl2009-TheLibraryStudyAtFresno-Ethnography.pdf.

Department for Business, Innovation and Skills (2011) *Higher Education: students at the heart of the system*, White Paper, Cm 8122.

Doiron, R. and Asselin, M. (2011) Exploring a New Learning Landscape in Tertiary Education, *New Library World*, **112** (5/6), 222-35.

Education Advisory Board (2011) *Redefining the Academic Library: managing the migration to digital information services*, University Leadership Council.

Eigenbrodt, O. (2008) Societal Places: the constitution of library space through activity. In *World Library and Information Congress: 74th IFLA General Conference and Council, Quebec, 10-14 August 2008*, International Federation of Library Associations and Institutions.

Foster, N. F. and Gibbons, S. (2007) *Studying Students: the Undergraduate Research Project at the University of Rochester*, Chicago: Association of College and Research Libraries.

Fraser, K. (2009) *Investigating How the Theory of Change Approach Can Inform the Evaluation of a Learning Apace: Sheffield University's Information Commons, a study submitted in partial fulfilment of the requirements for the degree of Master of Arts in Librarianship at the University of Sheffield*, University of Sheffield.

Freeman, G. T. (2005) The Library as Place: changes in learning patterns, collections, technology and use. In Smith, K. (ed.), *Library as Place: rethinking roles, rethinking space*, Council on Library and Information Resources.

Frischer, B. (2005) The Ultimate Internet Café: reflections of a practicing digital humanist about designing a future for the research library in the digital age. In Smith, K. (ed.), *Library as Place: rethinking roles, rethinking space*, Council on Library and Information Resources.

Gayton, J. T. (2008) Academic Libraries: 'social' or 'communal?' The nature and future of academic libraries, *The Journal of Academic Librarianship*, **34** (1), 60-6.

Hunley, S. and Schaller, M. (2009) Assessment: the key to creating spaces that promote learning, *EDUCAUSE Review*, **44** (2), 26-35.

Hunter, B., Lidgy, J. and Robert, G. (2005) Study of Critical Success Factors in the Strategic Development and Implementation of Innovative Learning Spaces and Related Learning Technologies. In Richards, G. (ed.), *Proceedings of World Conference on E-Learning in Corporate, Government, Healthcare, and Higher Education 2005*, AACE: Association for the Advancement of Computing in Education.

Hunter, G. and Ward, D. (2011) Students Research the Library: using student-led ethnographic research to examine the changing role of campus libraries, *College & Research Libraries News*, **72** (5), 264-8.

Joint Information Systems Committee (JISC) (2006) *Designing Spaces for Effective Learning: a guide to 21st Century learning space design*, JISC.

Joint Information Systems Committee (JISC) (2011) *Library Impact Data Project*, www.jisc.ac.uk/whatwedo/programmes/inf11/activitydata/libraryimpact.aspx.

Joint Information Systems Committee (JISC) (n.d.) *Developing Digital Literacies*, www.jisc.ac.uk/developingdigitalliteracies.

Joint Information Systems Committee (JISC) Infonet (n.d.) *Planning and Designing Technology Rich Learning Spaces: Glasgow Caledonian University, the Saltire Centre*, www.jiscinfonet.ac.uk/infokits/learning-space-design/more/case-studies/gcu.

Keating, S. and Gabb, R. (2005) *Putting Learning into the Learning Commons: a literature review*, Victoria University.

Keeling, R. (2004) *Learning Reconsidered: a campus-wide focus on the student experience*, National Association of Student Personnel Administrators, American College Personnel Association.

Learn Higher Centre for Excellence in Teaching and Learning (CETL) (2010) *Final*

Evaluation Report, Higher Education Academy,
http://learnhigher.ac.uk/resources/files/Stories/Final%20evaluation%20
report%20March%202010.pdf.

Lefebre, R. and Bashir, H. (2011) *Student Engagement Final Report: exploring student understandings of belonging on campus*, Higher Education Academy and University of Bradford.

Lewis, D. (2007) A Strategy for Academic Libraries in the First Quarter of the 21st Century, *College and Research Libraries*, **68** (5), 418–34.

Light, G. and Cox, R. (2001) *Learning and Teaching in Higher Education: the reflective professional*, Paul Chapman Publishing.

Lippincott, J. (2006) Linking the Information Commons to Learning. In Oblinger, D. (ed.), *Learning Spaces*, EDUCAUSE.

Lippincott, J. (2009) Learning spaces: involving faculty to improve pedagogy, *EDUCAUSE Review*, **44** (2), March/April, 16–25.

McLaughlin, P. and Mills, A. (2008) Where Shall the Future Student Learn? Student expectations of university facilities for teaching and learning. In *Preparing for the Graduate of 2015: Proceedings of the 17th Annual Teaching Learning Forum, Curtin University of Technology*, Curtin University of Technology.

Nagata, H. (2009) New 'Ba' (Locale) in Academic Libraries: information commons and learning commons, *Annals of Nagoya University Library Studies*, **7** (1), 3–14.

Neary, M. et al. (2010) *Learning Landscapes in Higher Education: clearing pathways, making spaces, involving academics in the leadership, governance and management of academic spaces in higher education*, University of Lincoln.

Nitecki, D. (2011) Space Assessment as a Venue for Defining the Academic Library, *Library Quarterly*, **81** (1), 27–59.

Oblinger, D. G. and Oblinger, J. L. (2005) Is It Age or IT: first steps toward understanding the net generation. In Oblinger, D. G. and Oblinger, J. L. (eds), *Educating the Net Generation*, EDUCAUSE.

Pearshouse, I. et al. (2009) *JISC Study of Effective Evaluation Models and Practices for Technology Supported Physical Learning Spaces Project (JELS): final report*, Joint Information Systems Committee.

Prensky M. (2001) Digital Natives, Digital Immigrants, Part 1, *On the Horizon*, **9** (5), 1–6.

Radcliffe, D. (2008) A Pedagogy-Space-Technology (PST) Framework for Designing and Evaluating Learning Places. In Radcliffe, D. et al. (eds), *Learning Spaces in Higher Education: positive outcomes by design*, University of Queensland, www.uq.edu.au/nextgenerationlearningspace/proceedings.

Ramsden, P. (2008) *The Future of Higher Education: teaching and the student experience*, Department for Innovation, Universities and Skills.

Ranseen, E. (2002) The Library as Place: changing perspectives, *Library Administration and Management*, **16**, Fall, 204.

Ray, K. L. (2002) The Postmodern Library in an Age of Assessment. In *ACRL Tenth National Conference, March 15-18, 2001, Denver*, Association of College and Research Libraries.

Roberts, S. and Weaver, M. (2006) Spaces for Learners and Learning: evaluating the impact of technology-rich learning spaces, *New Review of Academic Librarianship*, **12** (2), 95-107.

Rowlands, I. and Nicholas, D. (2008) *Information Behaviour of the Researcher of the Future: a CIBER Briefing Paper commissioned by the British Library and Joint Information Systems Committee*, Centre for Information Behaviour and the Evaluation of Research.

Somerville, M. and Collins, L. (2008) Collaborative Design: a learner-centred library planning approach, *The Electronic Library*, **26** (6), 803-20.

Tom, J. S. C., Voss, K. and Scheetz, C. (2008) The Space is the Message: first assessment of a learning studio, *EDUCAUSE Quarterly*, **31** (2), 42-52.

Towlson. K. and Pillai, M. (2008) Librarians and Learning Developers Working Together at De Montfort University Library, *SCONUL Focus*, **44**, 23-6.

Twait, M. (2009) If They Build It, They Will Come, *College & Research Libraries News,* **70** (1), 21-4.

UK Higher Education Space Management Group (UKSMG) (2006) *Space Utilization: practice, performance and guidelines*, UKSMG.

University of Auckland (n.d.) *Information Commons Group*, www.library.auckland.ac.nz/about-us/information-commons.

University of Bolton (n.d.) *Social Learning Zone*, www.bolton.ac.uk/Students/LifeAndLeisure/SocialLearningZone.aspx.

University of Bradford (2011) *Student Central: it's all under a brand new roof*, www.brad.ac.uk/studentcentral.

University of Cumbria (n.d.) *Carlisle Fusehill Street: Learning Gateway*, www.cumbria.ac.uk/StudentLife/VirtualTours/Home.aspx.

University of Exeter (n.d.) *The Forum: about the Forum Project*, www.exeter.ac.uk/forum/about.

University of Manchester (n.d.) *Alan Gilbert Learning Commons*, www.library.manchester.ac.uk/aboutus/projects/aglc.

University of Massachusetts Amherst (n.d.) *UMassAmherst Learning Commons*, www.library.umass.edu/learningcommons.

University of Portsmouth (n.d.) *General Information: choose your learning space*, www.port.ac.uk/lookup/generalinformation/learningspaces.

University of Sheffield (n.d.) *Information Commons*, www.sheffield.ac.uk/infocommons.

University of Sunderland (n.d.) *University Library Services: silent spaces*, http://library.sunderland.ac.uk/learning-spaces/silent-spaces/catherine-cookson-room.

Wilson, G. and Randall, M. (2012) The Implementation and Evaluation of a New

Learning Space: a pilot study, *Research in Learning Technology*, **20**, www.researchinlearningtechnology.net/index.php/rlt/article/view/14431.

9 Collaborative service provision through super-convergence

Maxine Melling, University of Gloucestershire, UK
(This chapter relates to the author's experience as Director of Library and Student Support at Liverpool John Moores University.)

Introduction and background

Traditionally, large organizations operate through structured units with a common focus and organized around budget and reporting lines. This use of infrastructure allows people working in organizations to maintain a span of control that makes sense to them and their colleagues, allowing the organization to manage its resource effectively. However, it's only a small step from developing these internal, necessary conveniences to presenting the organization to customers and stakeholders as if the reporting and budget lines represent the true nature of the organization. The stakeholder's perspective can become lost and they are expected to understand and navigate internal boundaries that have little relevance to their needs and interests. As Mark Clark has written,

> Users [of services] know what they need but fail to categorise the support needed and to differentiate between silos. (Clark, 2005, 160)

This comment appears to suggest a failure of necessary understanding by service users. However, organizations should seek to present services in ways that mirror user needs rather than in a way that demonstrates how the organization chooses to manage itself. Users then have no need to understand or differentiate between internal organizational boundaries (silos).

This tension between organizational infrastructure and service-user needs has been recognized by large public service providers, and there are good examples in the UK of how local councils in particular have sought to present public services in a seamless way, including the Life Centre provided by Wigan County Council (see www.wigan.gov.uk/Services/CouncilDemocracy/WiganLifeCentre). Similar developments have also taken place in some UK universities through the creation of 'super-converged' service departments, which seek to present student support from the student's point of view.

The first recorded use of the term super-convergence to describe service team structures is in the notes of a meeting of academic library service directors in early 2009 (Heseltine et al., 2009). The directors had met to consider a relatively recent phenomenon – the bringing together of a significant number of different services to form a multiply converged 'super' service team. They were seeking to explore whether this development in service provision was a passing fad or a growing trend, as well as wishing to share experiences in order to identify and develop best practice in leading such services. Since that first discussion there has been a growing trend towards super-convergence in UK higher education, with about 30 services now existing that might be described as super-converged.

The specific local drivers that have influenced the decision to adopt super-convergence are probably as many as are the institutions that have chosen to move in this direction. However, what is clear is that it is one increasingly common institutional response to the issues described in this volume of essays and may offer exciting opportunities for service improvement at a time when student expectations are high and competition for resources is strong. This chapter seeks to explore the drivers influencing this development, to consider the varying models of super-convergence and to offer a commentary on the challenges and opportunities facing leaders of super-converged services, with examples provided and with particular reference to the author's then service team at Liverpool John Moores University (LJMU).

The different models of super-convergence are discussed later this chapter. However, the broad definition of a super-converged service is taken to be where higher education providers

> bring together a range of support activities that are generally focussed on student support and are structurally converged. In some institutions these super-converged services are supported by a common help-desk and are sometimes provided from one building. (Heseltine et al., 2009, 122)

Drivers

Super-convergence in the UK has taken place during a period in which the focus on the student experience has become of vital importance to higher education providers and in which government initiatives have placed particular pressures on institutions. Graham Bulpitt discusses both these sector-wide drivers in his introductory chapter to a Leadership Foundation in Higher Education (LFHE) publication, which considers super-convergence in the context of improving the student experience (Bulpitt, 2012). Bulpitt highlights the deterioration in economic conditions in the UK since 2008 and the publication, in 2010, of the government White Paper, *Higher Education: students at the heart of the system* (Department for Business, Innovation and Skills, 2011), which sets out fundamental changes to the higher education sector. In particular the White Paper introduced full fees for undergraduate students recruited from September 2012 and an overt focus on market information to put students into the position of 'discerning customers'. As Bulpitt explains, the stated underlying principle behind the government's proposals was to make institutions more responsive by giving students a greater influence in the market, with assistance from enhanced market information on courses, assessment methods, graduate salaries and so on (HEFCE, 2011). This focus on the student as consumer can be seen as part of a broader emphasis on what is commonly called 'the student voice', seeking to involve students more actively in decision-making, working in partnership with the institution.

Bulpitt's argument is that super-converged services have been developed in order to provide a streamlined one-stop shop that can be seen to answer greater student pressure for customer service and can deliver cost-effectiveness through economies of scale. This argument is sound and is supported by several of the case studies in the LFHE report. At an LFHE meeting on 25 April 2012 Bulpitt acknowledged, however, that there have been a range of additional drivers, often local to an institution, and has also said that this move may reflect a willingness in the UK to experiment with different approaches.

Local drivers are often and inevitably linked to local opportunities and threats. In considering the convergence between IT and library services, which became established in UK universities in the 1980s, Field argued that

> the structural implementation of convergence will owe much to the local political, cultural, financial and spatial circumstances of any given institution.
>
> (Field, 2001, 272)

In other words, whatever the sectoral drivers, local context is everything. An institution needs to be culturally attuned to the very different ways of working required when structural boundaries are breached. The local politics need to support the change – with the vice-chancellor's buy-in often being critical to successful implementation. Other local drivers might be a decision to develop larger management portfolios, moving to a cabinet style of governance; to save money; or to balance the power of professional services teams and faculties. Very simple opportunistic events such as the retirement of a senior member of staff can also either be a driver or at least remove an obstacle to implementation. It is probably also worth considering the likelihood of vice-chancellors bumping into each other at a conference and being impressed with a new idea. Often the decision to restructure and to present services in a more innovative way is affected by the opportunities provided by the development of iconic new spaces. As the benefits of super-convergence are starting to become apparent some institutions are investing in physical space that enables and showcases the removal of boundaries and the seamless provision of service. The Forum building at the University of Exeter is a good example of this approach, where an iconic new building has been developed to bring all key services together and to act as a flagship for the University's student-centred vision (see www.exeter.ac.uk/about/campus/forum).

The initial driver that eventually led to super-convergence at LJMU was a desire to improve the student experience of administrative services by ensuring their seamless and professional delivery. There was a recognition that students were required to navigate between numerous service points, be they in the library, a school or faculty office or a central student administration service. All these service points offered different and valuable services but there was also quite considerable overlap in coverage and different practices in delivery and support.

Although the enhancement of the student experience was the key driver for change at LJMU, it was agreed that in addressing these issues and bringing all services together under one roof there would also be an opportunity to make some cost savings through delivering economies of scale and by removing duplication of activities. The initial investigation into the student experience of administration did not envisage the development of a super-converged service or the inclusion of library and IT support services in the mix. However, the library buildings, which enjoyed very long opening hours and were centrally located at each of the University's main campuses, became seen as a convenient home for a one-stop shop. Some internal and unplanned staff changes also occurred and the so-called super-converged department was developed. The term 'super-convergence' was only coined after the creation of the model and the term is never likely to be a term used when describing services to students.

Types of super-convergence, models and approaches

Models of super-convergence vary in both management approach and content. The general trend is to bring together a range of support activities that are broadly focused on student support and are structurally converged or offered in a seamless way that seeks to disguise structural separation. Most super-converged services aim to provide a single help desk or help service and, where physically possible, are provided from one building – usually the university library. Although the term 'one-stop shop' is less popular than it once was, the general approach is to bring all aspects of student support together in order to streamline provision.

One interesting aspect of super-convergence is the flexibility offered either to create a single line management of all areas of service included or to maintain different line management but still to present the services as a seamless whole. As long as local culture allows staff to work together effectively, regardless of line management, and the service is seen as seamless by the users, there is an argument that either approach is equally effective. The main issue that needs to be considered is that of customer service – ensuring that standards are clearly articulated and agreed regardless of the line management of the individuals employed.

The types of services that are brought together through super-convergence tend to be those that are student-facing or that support student-facing activity. The initial investigation of super-convergence in 2009 provided a list of the services that are usually included. These are:

- Library
- IT, including infrastructure, services and support
- Multimedia/learning objects creation
- Reprographics,
- Classroom support
- VLE [virtual learning environment] support
- Student administrative support, including registration and fees payments
- Course management, including submission of assignments
- Programme and module advice to students
- Student support services including counselling, PDP (Personal Development Planning), careers and employability, chaplaincy
- Academic skills for students, including IT and information skills/study skills
- Educational learning development/staff development activities in support of academic staff
- Advice to staff and students around issues such as copyright and plagiarism.

(Heseltine et al., 2009, 122)

Although there are examples where all or most of the services listed have been brought together under one structure, it is more common for a subset to be converged – representing the specific local drivers or focus of the institution. Figure 9.1 on the next page illustrates the most common groupings, which tend to be around student support, IT and systems or learning support. This figure shows the library as the common denominator, in recognition of the fact that super-converged services tend to include, and have sometimes been created around, the university library service. There are a number of reasons why this has been the case, including the central location and flexibility of university library buildings and the extended opening hours offered. University libraries

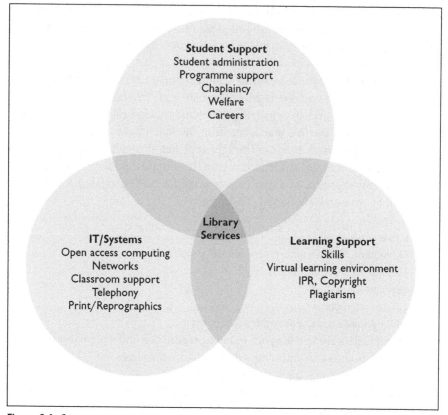

Figure 9.1 *Common service groupings for super-converged services*

have often already converged with IT services or with learning support services, providing a base for further development and experience of the issues involved. Librarians might also point out that their services are recognized to be very customer-focused and to do consistently well in user surveys such as the National Student Survey. As Dole, Hurych and Koehler (2000, 286) have argued, 'service to patron' is recognized as a primary value held by academic librarians. Certainly a customer focus is essential to the successful implementation of super-convergence.

The model of super-convergence adopted at LJMU brings all generic student facing services into one physical place. Most of the services are line managed by a service department called Library and Student Support (L&SS), which operates from three campus based centres as well as over the web. However, the centres also house staffed services provided by professionals in careers, employability, student advice and well-being, with appointments and referrals to these specialists being provided by L&SS reception staff. The centres therefore provide:

- *Library and learning resources*: including collection management, digitization, circulation, purchasing, licensing, copyright support, information literacy, research support, archives, study support and academic liaison.
- *ICT support*: including open access PCs and peripherals, open access copying and printing, laptop loans, help with IT and IT training.
- *Student services*: including enrolment of students, student finance support, coursework submission, withdrawals and module registration.
- *Programme advice*: including answering enquiries about the administration of the programme and referral to faculties for academic support.
- *Student advice and well-being*: including advice on disability support, finance, health, accommodation and support for international students.
- *Information on careers and employability*: including one-to-one careers advice, CV planning, qualifications and career planning.

At LJMU the ground floor of each centre was remodelled as a 'Student Zone', which provides a reception, appointment and referrals service; desk services providing transactional activity (e.g. finance support, handing in of coursework); advice on programme administration including enrolment and registration; bookable study rooms; open access PCs and other IT facilities; social learning areas; and self-service facilities (e.g. borrowing and return of books, printing, copying, scanning and vending services). These areas are staffed by people who have specialist skills in library, IT or student administration but share a number of core duties when working in the Student Zone. Staff operate from a reception area, a service desk and as rovers. Specialist services, which include welfare advice, careers advice and help with learner support (e.g. literature searching), are provided from elsewhere in the centres, with referral and appointments managed by staff in the Student Zone. The core library services (printed stock, study support, etc.) are also housed in the centres, but away from the Student Zones. The Zones are open 24 hours a day during semester, offering staffed support for 15 of those hours and self-service facilities overnight.

One of the main aspirations of the changes was that students would not need to visit lots of different buildings in order to receive support with their studies and the administration of their course. Since the changes were made, the number of visits to the centres (i.e. gate counts) has remained relatively constant but headcount in the centres has increased year on year – with a 12% increase in year 1 and a 32% increase in year 2. This suggests that students who come into the centres are staying for very long periods because they have no need to go elsewhere unless they are attending lectures and seminars or seeking academic advice and support, all of which are available in the relevant faculty building.

Although models of super-convergence vary, this author believes that a service can only truly be seen as super-converged if the changes made impact directly upon the way in which the service is delivered to and perceived by students. If a university has drawn all student-facing services under the line management of a senior member of staff but continues to present them to students from separate places and using different customer-service standards, then the change is one of line management and not one of delivery and is more akin to a pro-vice-chancellor's approach to portfolio management. The student continues to be asked to navigate internal, necessary conveniences of budget and line management control and the service does not mirror the student's needs and perceptions. There are examples of super-convergence in the sector where services continue to be offered from different buildings simply because the available space doesn't allow the physical co-location of services in any one place. In these instances extra effort needs to be made to 'badge' the different services consistently and to present common service standards.

Key issues
Leadership

In recent years the term 'cold climate' has been used by a number of commentators to describe a situation where change is so extreme that learnt skills and behaviours are of little or no help in deciding future options. Professor David Eastwood, Vice-Chancellor of the University of Birmingham, introduced this phrase into LFHE discussions about the requirements placed on future leaders in the sector, with a debate title 'Leadership in a Cold Climate: leading where the past is no reliable guide to the future' (Eastwood, 2011). The term is particularly relevant when considering the individual or management-team approaches needed to develop and lead a super-converged service effectively. In leading such a service it is necessary to develop innovative ways of working, often without the benefit of benchmarking with other service providers or of using established data to evidence decision-making. Leaders of these services may not be familiar with the culture or working methods of subsets of staff in their service or with the wider networks associated with the various professional groupings. In addition, it is very unlikely that the super-converged department will have statistical measures that cover all aspects of the work or established trends analysis with which to evidence decisions or to make a case for resources. When taking over responsibility for a new area, practice amongst many professionals is to seek support from peer groups. Again, this may be challenging when no such group exists.

Of course, many established leadership skills are still necessary in order to lead a multiply converged service and there is experience across the sector of leading service teams that are converged in some form or another. It's interesting to look at the list of qualities provided by Hanson in his critique of IT/library convergence, which includes a number of important attributes for leaders of these services – all of which are directly relevant to people seeking to lead a super-converged service. These include:

- Commitment to the model
- Clear strategy and goals
- Customer focus
- Good communications and listening
- Genuine appreciation of what all members of the converged group can contribute
- Ability to build and motivate cross sectional teams
- Being a university person first and a librarian or IT professional second.

(Hanson, 2005, 7)

The last criterion in this list, that of being a university person first and a professional from a specific area second, is of particular interest. Most director or head-of-service posts assume a knowledge of the service area being led that has been developed over several years of work as a professional in that sphere. Networks have usually been built within a particular profession and the director is expected to be able to engage with staff in some detail about developments. Mark Clark, in discussing library and IT convergence, went as far as to argue that a successful director has to have full comprehension of the breadth of his or her service and that this is not possible in a converged department (Clark, 2005, 157). Graham Bulpitt referenced this belief in his own commentary on super-convergence:

> The move away from traditional structures can undermine the relationship between responsibilities and expertise. Conventional practice has been for a departmental director to have followed a traditional career route, gaining experience in that specialism. The portfolios associated with converged services, and also with cabinet government, mean that individuals will have responsibilities which go beyond their core professional experience. (Bulpitt, 2012, 40)

These arguments are often at the centre of leadership of large converged services and of super-converged services. The final decision regarding whether or not the leader of a service needs to understand the detail of all aspects of their service team may also be dependent upon the nature of the parent organization. How much does the parent organization look to the director of service to act as a senior leader within and across the organization and how much does it require the director to be a technical professional who operates within a contained sphere?

Another critical issue is, of course, the director's own senior team. In order to lead a super-converged service effectively the director needs team members who represent the various professional specialisms included in the structure and who are able to work openly and effectively in a team that includes other specialist areas. All members of the team need to understand and appreciate the full range of areas included, looking at how their own area of responsibility can work most effectively within the whole. It is very important that the director trusts their specialist managers to be experts in their own field so that they can give informed advice. The main role of the director then becomes that of having the ability to make a judgement about this advice whilst placing it within the broader needs of the whole service and the parent institution.

It can be argued that if the detailed professional knowledge lies with managers who report into the service director then there is a chance that one or more areas lose status in the university. To date the majority of directors of super-converged services have come from a professional library background. This means that they tend to be seen by the institution as both the university librarian and the director of the larger service and are able to represent the needs of the library at university committee level. Should the director's background be in one of the many other professional spheres included in a super-converged service (e.g. student services, student administration, computing) there is a challenge in relation to representation of the library and its needs in the university. This issue is raised not because the author of this chapter and most of the intended readers are professional librarians! It is raised because the role of the library in any university is a very particular one, linked closely to academic delivery and research support. If the service director is expected to represent the library institutionally, for example at the academic board, but does not have the requisite professional knowledge, there could be a slow decline in the library's status or strength. This concern does not mean that an argument is being made for librarians to be the obvious choice for directors of super-converged services, but rather that the issue of professional background and knowledge should be considered by institutions when choosing to introduce super-convergence. It is also important that the constituent parts of a super-converged service, such as the library or student services, are properly represented at institutional level and that the person responsible for this representation is clearly identified.

Staffing and staff skills

One of the critical success factors in developing effective super-converged services is in the balance achieved between the core or generalist skills and specialist skills held by the front-facing staff. This balance is not constant. Generalist skills can become extremely complex, requiring specialist teams to provide them, while services that previously required specialist knowledge can be made more straightforward, for example through the introduction of intuitive IT systems and self-service. It is therefore necessary to keep the staff skills-base under regular review and to support staff when necessary in changing and developing their skills.

Staff providing front-facing enquiry support to users of super-converged services need to be confident 'advanced generalists' who have highly developed customer-care skills and sufficient knowledge to handle initial questions, knowing when to refer them on to the second level of support. This requirement has been identified by a number of directors of super-converged services, including Robert Hall, Director at King's College London, who has referred to 'the notion of a new professional role: "generalist staff"' (2012, 8).

For the first year of super-convergence at LJMU the staff providing front-line support maintained their pre-existing roles and specialisms. Job descriptions were kept the same and the key front-facing specialist services were offered from different service desks in the Student Zone. The over-riding driver for this approach was the speed with which the development of the service took place – over a relatively short time span of nine months. However, the newly formed service was also taking on responsibilities that were new to everyone and therefore carried some additional challenges and risks. A decision was therefore taken to concentrate the available staff-development time on change-management training and skills training for the new responsibilities. It was agreed that this represented sufficient change for all staff and for service delivery, without seeking to go any further. This stepped approach also allowed all members of the service team to work in and test the new model so that future changes would be informed by real experience and student feedback.

After the first academic year as a super-converged service at LJMU a number of front-line staff expressed frustration that they were not able to help service users with some of the less complex enquiries outside their specialism. This resulted in the identification of 'core skills' that everyone felt able to support. The core duties include basic support work such as taking in coursework, resetting passwords, replacing student cards and making appointments. Specialist skills maintained by staff include student enrolment and assistance with programme enquiries (student administration staff) and IT support or helping with enquiries about circulation activities (research and learner-support staff). Training was carried out to enable all staff to provide this range of services and changes were made to the physical representation of the desk services – bringing all staff together at one service desk.

The gradual approach to change is illustrative of a desire to test the changes being introduced and to give people the opportunity to work within the new model in order to gain confidence before being asked to expand their skills base. This sort of gradual change can only be introduced if the integrity of the service model as experienced by service users is protected.

Culture, values, identity and boundaries
What is the culture of an organization?

At its simplest, the culture and values of an organization or of a team within an organization can be summed up as 'how we do things here'. At its more complex, the culture and values can be seen as beliefs, attitudes, customs and behaviours that have evolved over time and may have been influenced by key events or institutional battle scars, or have been formed by training and membership or association with a professional body. However they are defined, the strength of the culture and values of a team and the ways in which they influence the team's willingness to adopt different ways of working should not be underestimated when seeking to introduce any change management programme.

One might argue, and this author does, that success in any service organization is dependent upon a clear articulation and understanding of the values of that organization and the associated behaviours. However, this becomes even more important when developing a super-converged team. One of the real challenges is in understanding the value systems of the different teams or professional groupings brought together and the ways in which customer service is understood and defined by those teams.

In addition to impacting on approaches to customer support, values and culture can also have deeply embedded influences on how people organize their working day. In considering convergence of library and IT services, Sutton (2000) referred to aspects of library hierarchies being 'uncongenial' to IT staff. Although there's a temptation to fall into easy stereotypes (controlling librarian/lone-wolf IT worker), it is helpful to find ways of exposing people's preferred ways of doing business and being as open as possible about what internal differences can be accommodated and when a compromise - or new way of doing things - needs to be found.

Practical ways of discussing organizational values

At LJMU the challenges associated with the possible difference in values and cultures were addressed in two distinct ways. First, a change management programme was devised for all the staff coming together to form the new service department. This programme included the following workshops:

- *Getting to know you*: introductory workshops in which staff were able to exchange experiences and develop an awareness and understanding of each other's areas of expertise.
- *Managing yourself through change*: workshops for all staff to understand the theory, practicalities and personal realization of the change process.
- *Managing others through change*: workshops for all managers and supervisors to help envisage change from the perspective of their team members and support them through the process.
- *Customer service training*: refresher workshops for all front-facing staff, with an explanation of the customer-service standards for the team.
- *Skills training*: focusing on new skills being picked up by the team following its creation.
- *Coaching and mentoring*: for all staff in a supervisory role to enable them to mentor staff, particularly with regards to the service values and culture.

The second approach taken was a large-scale project to identify and articulate the values and culture of the new team and to identify behaviours for all staff which were associated with those values. This project involved use of the 'Cultural Web' (MindTools) approach to identifying elements that describe or influence organization culture (Cultural Web, n.d.) to engage with staff from the team and with key stakeholder groups, including senior managers from the university, students, other service teams and academics. The agreed values and behaviours have been presented to service users as two 'promises' with associated staff behaviours and service standards.

Examples (not a comprehensive list) of one of the promises and the associated behaviours identified are shown here:

Promise: To provide support services to the highest standard we can achieve, students and staff at the centre of our business.

To see the service from your point of view:
- Treat each of you as we would like to be treated
- Acknowledge your name, where appropriate
- Avoid jargon

Aim to satisfy your needs by:
- Going the extra mile
- Being clear about what you can expect from us
- Building on our traditional strengths and good practice

(Taken with permission from the LJMU Library and Student Support Values Statement, www.ljmu.ac.uk/lea/115593.htm)

This promise is supported by service standards which include:

Measure performance and benchmark against best practice through:
- Using statistics and feedback to inform services
- Ensuring we talk to you and collaborate on how the service is provided
- Giving feedback to you about our performance and how we've responded to your comments
- Setting our own standards of best practice and telling you about them.

Professional identity and the role of the professional associations

The staff working in the range of services that tend to be brought together in super-converged services are represented by a number of different professional associations, which are discussed by Raegan Hiles and Andrew West in Chapter 3 of this volume of essays. Traditionally, the professional associations have assisted members with issues including leadership development, staff skills, statistics and impact measures and lobbying. All of these issues are critically important to leaders and other professional staff working within super-converged services, but there are many instances when they need to be considered across the various professional boundaries rather than in relation to a university administrator, librarian, student adviser or systems specialist.

In October 2010 a conference entitled 'Super-convergence' was hosted at LJMU, which was attended by over 60 delegates from a range of different professional backgrounds. One of the outcomes of this event was a decision to produce a briefing paper for the relevant professional associations – SCONUL (the Society of College, National and University Libraries, AMOSSHE, The Student Services Organisation, the Academic Registrars Council and the Universities and Colleges Information Systems Association (UCISA) – advising them of the key concerns of members and seeking support (Melling, Selby and Hiles, 2011). This paper suggested a specific role for the professional associations, which included:

- supporting more formal networking opportunities and relationship building between professional groups
- leading on the development of new performance and impact measures for super-converged services
- examining the development of relevant tools and customer satisfaction methodologies.

The executive boards of the five associations all considered the paper and some have held discussions about the ways in which super-converged teams might be better supported. In addition, staff development events and conferences have included discussion of the issue.

The LFHE has also identified the need to support leaders of super-converged services, hence the recent LFHE report (Bulpitt, 2012) and networking events on 'Leading the Whole Student Experience'.

These early explorations can only be a positive move and do provide a forum for discussion and support during a period of rapid change. However, just as leaders of converged library and IT departments have always needed to negotiate membership between SCONUL and UCISA, it appears that leaders of super-converged services have had to add networking across an increased number of professional associations onto their list of responsibilities. Innovative thinking is still needed to consider how boundaries are truly broken down between the professional associations to ensure that a subset of their own members are not expected to navigate 'necessary conveniences of structure' as our students were before super-convergence took place.

Conclusion

In a recent LFHE publication the authors state:

> Collaboration is a necessary response to 21st century operating conditions and the appearance of multi-faceted challenges and goals.
>
> (Levitt, Goreham and Diepeveen, 2011, 3)

The super-convergence of student-facing service teams is one such response, taken by a growing number of universities. Evaluation of this approach is in its infancy and is challenging because of the different approaches taken across the sector. There is a clear need to embed monitoring and evaluation into the model and to develop robust impact measures. At LJMU, usage figures suggest that the model is popular with students, and feedback, although only anecdotal at this stage, supports this assessment. Comments by students in the National Student Survey (NSS) after the first year of operation included:

> The improvements to the Library in the last couple of years have meant that I can now easily spend all day working here.

and

> The student experience has truly been enhanced as a result of all student facing services being under one roof, and the staff there being able to support students using the service in an excellent manner.

Of course, any approach to service models or to the structuring of professional service teams needs to be relevant to the local culture and strategic priorities of the host institution, and super-convergence is not necessarily appropriate to all universities. However, it is an approach that removes the need for service users to understand internal boundaries, seeking to provide services in a way that reflects the users' perspective and convenience rather than those of the organization.

References

Bulpitt, G. (ed.) (2012) *Leading the Student Experience: super-convergence of organisation, structure and business process*, Series 3, Publication 5, Leadership Foundation for Higher Education.

Clark, M. (2005) Choosing Not to Converge: Manchester University. In Hanson, T. (ed.), *Managing Academic Support Services in Universities: the convergence experience*, Facet Publishing.

Cultural Web (n.d.) *Cultural Web: aligning your organization's culture with strategy*, www.mindtools.com/pages/article/newsSTR_90.htm.

Department for Business, Innovation and Skills (2011) *Higher Education: students at the heart of the system*, White Paper, Cm 8122, www.bis.gov.uk/assets/biscore/higher-education/docs/h/11-944-higher-education-students-at-heart-of-system.pdf.

Dole, W. V., Hurych, J. M. and Koehler, W. C. (2000) Values for Librarians in the Information Age: an expanded examination, *Library Management*, **21** (6) 285-97.

Eastwood, D. (2011) A New Deal for HE: round table debate, *Engage*, Summer, **26**, 4.

Field, C. (2001) Theory and Practice: reflections on convergence in UK universities, *Liber Quarterly*, **11** (3), 267-89.

Hall, R. (2012) Towards a New Model of Integrating the Student Experience. In Bulpitt, G. (ed.), *Leading the Student Experience: super-convergence of organisation, structure and business process*, Series 3, Publication 5, Leadership Foundation for Higher Education.

Hanson, T. (ed.) (2005) *Managing Academic Support Services in Universities: the convergence experience*, Facet Publishing.

HEFCE, (2011) *Key Information Sets*, www.hefce.ac.uk/learning/infohe/kis.htm.

Heseltine, R., Marsh, S., McKnight, S. and Melling, M. (2009) Super-convergence: SCONUL shared experience meeting, 16 February 2009, *SCONUL Focus*, **46**, 121-4.

Levitt, R., Goreham, H. and Diepeveen, S. (2011) *Higher Education Collaborations: implications for leadership, management and governance: final report*, Series 3, Publication 1, Leadership Foundation for Higher Education Research and Development.

Melling, M., Selby, E. and Hiles, R. (2011) *Super-Convergence: briefing note to professional bodies, January*, unpublished.

Sutton, A. M. (2000) *Convergence: a review of the literature*. In Reid, B. J. and Foster, W. (eds), *Achieving Cultural Change in Networked Libraries*, Gower.

10 Joint-use libraries and transformational change

Ruth Kifer, San José State University, USA

Introduction

Joint-use libraries are created between public (also known as community) libraries and university libraries; between public schools and public libraries; between community colleges and universities; and between any library organizations wishing to collaborate on the delivery of library services. These collaborations exist as a result of institutions of higher education and other entities making the bold decision to work across organizational boundaries for the benefit of their library communities to make best use of limited resources. The joint organizations that are created embrace a broader view of mission and vision than do organizations with a more traditional and sometimes insular view of their reason for being. Joint-use libraries exist with a variety of different models of administration and funding, of varying sizes and in different geographic locations.

In August 2003 the 475,000 square foot (44,000 square meters) Dr Martin Luther King, Jr. Library (King Library), a joint-use library created by San José State University (SJSU) and the City of San José, opened to serve their respective communities. The grand opening was met with applause and rave reviews by the close to 12,000 people who were on hand for the festivities that day. As the ten-year anniversary looms (August 2013), the King Library has provided stellar library services, technological innovation and access to print and digital collections for the fifth largest campus in the California State University (CSU) system, the third largest city in California and the tenth largest city in the USA. A review of the planning process employed to develop this joint library and an exploration of the accompanying staffing issues, user perceptions, budgetary matters and other factors are instructive in understanding the operation of such a library. These observations can provide a foundation for predictions for the next ten years of collaboration in light of exponential technological advances, innovation in higher education and the 'new normal' of decreased tax-generated funding for public libraries and state-supported universities in the USA.

As the library enters the ninth year of operation of this collaboration, the joint venture has proven to be successful in meeting the mission of providing lifelong learning for the residents of San José, often referred to as the capital of Silicon Valley, and the university community. The planning for this partnership began in earnest in 1998, five years before its opening just prior to the start of the fall academic semester of 2003. The essence, composition and physical design of university libraries and public libraries alike will have evolved considerably by 2013, over 15 years later. What does it mean for this model of library collaboration? How will the partnership continue to grow and develop as the metamorphosis of the library as an institution in today's changing society progresses? This chapter examines these issues and charts the course for ongoing successful collaborations between university and public libraries as an effective and cost-efficient means in today's learning environments and volatile world economy.

The history of joint libraries

Libraries housed in schools that also serve the general public have existed in the USA since 1906 or even earlier (Bundy, 2003, 130). As of 2007, Australia had over 120 school–community libraries, and joint-use libraries can be found in Canada, the UK, China and Africa (McNicol, 2008, 3-4). Collaborations between major universities and large cities have not been as prevalent in the USA and those of significant size did not appear worldwide until the 1990s and early 2000s (Bundy, 2003, 135-6). A selected list of combined public–university libraries worldwide includes Harnosand, Sweden (Gomez, Hulthen ad Drehmer, 1998); Worcester Hive at the University of Worcester and Worcestershire County Council, UK (Keene and Fairman, 2011); Boland College of Education, Cape Peninsula University of Technology and the Cape Technikon libraries, Cape Town, South Africa (Moll, 2010); and Tritonia Academic Library, Vaasa/Abo Akademi Vaasa, Finland (Fleming, 2012).

In the USA numerous joint-use university–public libraries of varying sizes have been established since the beginning of the 21st century. Broward County, Florida, USA, and NOVA Southeastern University collaborated to open the joint-use Alvin Sherman Library, Research, and Information Technology Center in 2001. This is a merger of a large privately funded university library in a densely populated urban–suburban area of Florida. NOVA Southeastern University is responsible for managing the entire joint-library facility including the supervision of library staff and librarians who deliver specific public library services and have become university employees. Prior to opening the joint-use library, the university conducted a lengthy recruitment process and hired employees trained in public library services and collections as university employees. Although the operating agreement between the county and the university specifies NOVA Southeastern University as the sole owner of the joint-use library and requires the county to provide funding to support joint-use by the public (Office of the County Auditor, 2007, 3), all services, collections and programmes are open to all library users from both the university and the public communities (MacDougall and Quinlan, 2001, 134).

It should be noted that in the NOVA Broward County joint-use library, all library users can avail themselves of all the library has to offer while in the library facility, yet the management of the library operations is not merged in the same way as the management of the King Library in California. Therefore many of the administrative issues present in a merged-management model, such as the King Library, may not rise to the same level of complexity in the single-management model, such as the NOVA Broward County Library. However, as Harriett MacDougall, Director of the Library, has stated, many training and orientation issues were present when the organization recruited and hired professional and support staff at one time to provide services to both university and public library users in this new joint-use library (MacDougall and Quinlan, 2001, 139).

The joint-use Metropolitan University Library and the St Paul Bluff Branch Public Library opened in 2004 in St Paul Minnesota is an example of a joint-use library that could best be described as co-located, with the public library services and collections in a distinct area within the facility from that of the university, and with complete separation of public and university library departments. David Barton, Dean of the Metropolitan University Library, states: 'It took a long time for us to get to the point where members of the public could use university resources and members of the university community could use public library materials, and both groups could intermingle freely in one facility, but once we did, it proved successful from the outset and continues that way more than five years later' (Mudd and Havens, 2009, 7). In this scenario, library users affiliated with the university and those from the general public receive library services and access to collections in one facility; however, the management of the services and collections provided are clearly distinct from one library organization to the other.

An excellent selected listing of joint-use libraries located in many countries, including those located in the USA such as the Alvin Sherman Library, the Research and Information Technology Center in Florida, the Metropolitan State University/Dayton's Bluff Branch Library in St Paul Minneapolis and the King Library in San José California, discussed in the remainder of this chapter, can be found in Appendix I of Sarah McNicol's *Joint-Use Libraries: libraries for the future* (2008, 195).

Dr Martin Luther King, Jr. Library collaboration
Background

The City of San José, California, has a population of close to one million people and is situated in the high-tech corridor of the South San Francisco Bay region of Northern California, known as Silicon Valley. San José State University (SJSU), with an enrolment of over 30,000 students, is publicly funded as one of the 32 campuses of the CSU system that has a total of over 400,000 students state-wide. SJSU is the oldest public institution of higher education on the West Coast of the USA and draws students primarily from the County of Santa Clara in California with a smaller number of out-of-state and international students. The population of the City and SJSU is highly diverse with no one ethnicity constituting a majority. The population of the City is: 33.2% Hispanic, 31.7% Asian/Pacific Islander, 28.7% White, 2.9% African-American and 3.5% other. San José residents speak more than 56 different languages and less that 50% of the population speaks English in the home (City of San José, 2012, 2). The student population at SJSU is: 31.87% Asian, 26.85% White, 20.37% Hispanic, 3.87% African-American, 6.85% International, and 9.94% other (see SJSU website, SJSU Office of Institutional Research, 2012).

In 1996 both the City and SJSU needed new library facilities to address overcrowded conditions and inadequate wiring to allow for the growing use of technology to access collections and services. Then SJSU President, Dr Robert Caret, and then City Mayor, the Honorable Susan Hammer, discussed ways in which the City and SJSU could improve town–gown relations, while collaborating on a major facility project. They decided that a library would be a joint venture that could result in benefits for both the residents of the City and the students, faculty and students of the university. In 1998 the City and SJSU signed an operating agreement, and under the leadership of Dean of the University Library, Dr James Schmidt, and Director of the San José Public Library, Jane Light, planning for the joint-use library began. The memorandum of understanding (MOU) spelled out the elements of the joint venture to which the City and SJSU agreed. Details included staffing levels, technology enhancements, policy, procedures, use of the name of the library, the way to handle conflict, and operational issues. The MOU for the King Library can be found at: www.sjlibrary.org/files_king/documents/operating_agreement.pdf. After Dr Schmidt's retirement as dean, Dr Patricia Breivik was appointed dean in 1998 and with Light continued the in-depth planning process initiated by Schmidt.

Consultation in the planning for the joint-use library included conversations with the general public, the university faculty and staff of both libraries. Initial response to the idea of the City and SJSU collaboration on such a costly joint initiative was mixed at best. In an editorial piece, the *San José Mercury News*, the local newspaper, declared the plan for the joint-use library to be brilliant and that it could end up being the main accomplishment for which Mayor Susan Hammer would be remembered (San José Mercury News, 1997, 6B). At the other end of the spectrum, the SJSU faculty formed a group, Save Our University Library (SOUL), in opposition to the proposal. Faculty were concerned that public library users would check out so many scholarly books from the university collections that students and faculty would not have them available for their research, teaching and learning activities. Many library staff and librarians from both library organizations voiced concerns regarding the impending merger of the two large libraries in downtown San José. They were worried that such a merger would result in the loss of their identities as either public or university librarians. Some City residents objected to the collaboration, fearing that the money invested in this large joint-use library would take resources away from the neighbourhood branches, which experienced high use and were badly in need of renovation.

Planning

In order to build support for the library proposal a series of community meetings were held with presentations by SJSU, City staff and the architects so that the concept of the joint-use library could be explained and the anticipated benefits to the community better understood. The university academic senate held meetings to discuss the concerns that many faculty had about the project but eventually the academic senate voted to support the proposal (Thompson, 2004, 1-3). Over much time and with participation of library staff in multiple planning teams, many of the objections from librarians and other library workers were addressed. A senior core planning leadership team was formed and six joint planning teams made up of staff and librarians from both library organizations were developed. The teams covered administrative services, organizational design and development, collection management, technical services, policies, procedures and user services (Peterson, 2004, 35). The architects participated with the planning teams to glean input from staff of both organizations on aspects of the building design, including library user space and staff working areas. Both the public library and the university library hired project managers who oversaw the ongoing progress of the planning teams, ensuring that feedback from these groups was moved forward and that the issues specific to their home organization were included.

The planning teams and the discussions covered a range of topics including everything from whether the collections would be integrated even though they were in two different classification schemes, to whether food and drink would be permitted in public spaces. The question of whether there would be one or two reference desks drew extensive discussion, but after determining through a study in both existing libraries that the reference questions at the public library reference desk and the university library desk were more alike than different, it was determined that there would be one merged reference desk (Peterson, 2004, 34). The very time-consuming planning process ensured that decisions were made in consultation with appropriate people and this helped to engage and win over staff to the project.

Results

In August 2013, the King Library will have been open as a joint-use library for ten years. The university and public communities are proud of their unique and successful joint-use library, a hub for lifelong learning, culture and civic engagement, while the library staff and librarians are rewarded daily as they deliver access to information resources and services to the community. Ten years is a long time, particularly for libraries experiencing exponential change in the growth of technology and expectations of library users, and declining governmental financial support for public universities and libraries. Observations on the use of the library have shown that some of the assumptions made during the planning and design of the building were accurate but in many ways user needs have continued to evolve as library users have become more technology-savvy, information-sophisticated and consumer-conscious students of higher education.

If foot traffic alone were any indication, by all standards, the King Library has been a huge success. In a typical day during the Fall or Spring university semesters, the gate counts range from 12,000 to 15,000 visitors. However, total gate counts have dropped since 2009 (see Table 10.1 for statistics showing the decline of library gate counts). This may in part be due to a budget-demanded drop in

Table 10.1 Declining gate counts at the King Library	
Academic year	Totals
Aug. 2003 to June 2004	2,542,788
July 2004 to June 2005	2,661,157
July 2005 to June 2006	2,632,821
July 2006 to June 2007	2,628,273
July 2007 to June 2008	2,736,925
July 2008 to June 2009	2,726,636
July 2009 to June 2010	2,476,639
July 2010 to June 2011	2,426,912

Adapted with permission from San José University Library online statistics 2003–2012, unpublished.

university enrolments, but an increase in remote use of digital library resources has happened simultaneously. The use of the library from home, office and dorm room is now much greater than during the planning of the facility. Students still flock to the open-design, light and attractive building, whether for individual or group study and technology-driven learning activities. The library's 39 study rooms can be reserved by students and the public and all are always in use. The university has benefited from the joint venture with the City as evidenced by the ever visible student population on all floors of the library during the academic year. And, the public library users at the King Library have had far longer opening hours than is typically seen in public libraries in the USA and more opening hours than the San José neighbourhood branches. On opening at 8 a.m. each day there are students waiting for entry at the entrance of the library facing the university and city residents waiting at the doors that face downtown.

Since the King Library opened its doors, the City has built a new City Hall less than one block away, and the streets immediately surrounding the facility have seen the establishment of restaurants, residential facilities and commercial enterprises serving employees and customers of the library, the university and the City Hall. Although economic development has hit a plateau most recently, the urban area surrounding the joint-use library has grown considerably since the opening of the facility. Libraries have been characterized as urban anchor institutions, builders of social capital, and supporters of economic development (Kifer, 2007, 105), and this phenomenon in downtown San José demonstrates that the King Library has succeeded in this role.

Operations and services

Access to university and public library information resources, librarian expertise, library services and learning spaces is provided to all library users, reflecting the intentions of the designers of the joint-use library to be a centre of lifelong learning for residents of the City and SJSU. Although within the library different areas of the building are designated as university, City, common or shared space for management and budgeting purposes, all users are free to utilize all areas of the building and to charge out books, audio, video, and other media materials from any section of the building. The only exception to this is that, for safety reasons, only individuals accompanied by a child or who have a specific research project in children's literature can enter the children's room. The upper floors are teeming with university students bringing with them their laptops, e-tablets or smartphones, while floors offering desktop reservable computers are more popular with members of the general public. For SJSU students, laptop computers and iPads are available for hourly and weekly loan. This service is provided using student-generated revenue and so is one of the few services not available to all library users. Since the library's opening, the demand for desktop computers for public and student use has declined, as can be seen in Table 10.2.

Table 10.2 Decline in desk-top computer reservations at the King Library	
Academic year	Total
Aug. 2003 to June 2004	635,405
July 2004 to June 2005	742,205
July 2005 to June 2006	709,356
July 2006 to June 2007	708,322
July 2007 to June 2008	738,325
July 2008 to June 2009	818,736
July 2009 to June 2010	606,698
July 2010 to June 2011	489,785
July 2011 to June 2012	354,248

Adapted with permission from San José University Library online statistics, 2004–5 and 2010–12, unpublished.

The library reference desk is located on a shared floor, managed and staffed by university and public library staff and serves all library users. Usage statistics for the reference desk have dropped as they have in most US academic libraries, as students and other library users now use chat, e-mail and text reference services and many times conduct un-intermediated information searches. The service desk on the floor of the library that houses the general public library collection is staffed by public library staff, although student library users are welcomed at that desk and frequently use the public library non-fiction area to complete academic assignments. A heavily used public library collection is the foreign language collection, which has print, audio and video materials in over 20 languages available for loan. The diverse SJSU student population is drawn to this collection for language study and the opportunity to read material in their home language, as are all residents of San José, for whom the collection was conceived.

Four library instruction rooms, equipped with laptop or desktop computers, data projectors, smartboards and other technology for group instruction in the use of the library's close to 400 digital databases are shared spaces open to both communities. University librarians with liaison responsibilities to the university's 70 academic departments teach information literacy classes on appointment. The technology used in these classrooms is managed and maintained by the library's jointly managed and staffed information technology department.

The wide range of activities occurring in the library makes the environment very busy and often noisy. Students can elect to study on a 'quiet study only' or 'silent study only' floor or to work in groups on a floor alive with activity and noise. This can be confusing to a new library user who doesn't understand why he or she is hearing noise in a library and so staff frequently need to explain the range of study areas available. Young university students in an urban downtown library for the first time can be surprised and sometimes uncomfortable sharing space with homeless people or individuals with apparent mental illness who may use the library. This requires staff and librarians to be prepared to help library users understand the unique library in which they find themselves and assist in making all library users comfortable in a diverse environment.

The diversity of the library users at any given time goes well beyond ethnicity. University students regularly see toddlers on the way to story time; senior citizens attending adult library programmes or seeking assistance with tax preparation or legal issues; downtown business people using information resources; or members of the homeless population freely using the available computers, print information resources and comfortable seating. The partnership between the City and SJSU provides opportunities for joint programming to meet the information needs of the library users. An example of this is the partnership between the public library and the SJSU School of Social Work, which has resulted in the Social Workers in the Library Program (www.sjlibrary.org/event/social-workers-library), complementing the popular Lawyers in the Library Program (www.sjlibrary.org/event/lawyers-library). The Social Workers in the Library Program provides opportunities for graduate students to work directly with individuals who need social work services in a non-threatening library environment.

Three very popular services of the library that are used by both the general public and the university community are the exhibit spaces, study rooms and programme meeting rooms. The library has multiple exhibit areas that are available for members of the public or the university community to book free of charge for public exhibits of artwork and educational displays. These exhibit spaces have become very popular and exhibits are reserved up to two years in advance. University students, faculty and student organizations take advantage of this opportunity to show their creative work, and budding artists from the community of San José do the same. Study rooms may be booked by students and the general public for small group meetings of up to approximately eight people and are usually occupied at any given time. The library's two large meeting rooms require reservations for community and university programmes months in advance in order to find a room available. These spaces are very visible examples of the successful integration of the two communities and their enthusiastic use of the joint-use library services.

Evolving library user expectations

Two technology needs not anticipated during the planning of the library building include wireless access and a sufficient number of electrical outlets for portable devices. When the library opened in 2003 it was not equipped with a wireless system, but since then the university has provided wireless access for all library users. With the volume of activity in the library, the growth of portable smart devices and the estimated 2.5 portable devices per SJSU student, the current wireless system is overloaded and can be a source of user dissatisfaction. Plans are under way to provide a more powerful wireless system for the entire university, including all library users. In addition, the lack of a sufficient number of electrical outlets for people to charge their portable devices has steadily grown as more students and other library users bring their own portable devices with them to the library.

During the planning for the King Library it was decided that the digital presence of the library would be merged as well as the physical presence. The resulting website was a merged site with resources for both public library users and SJSU students and faculty integrated. Over the first five years this web design was maintained with minor modifications and updates. A redesign of the website was established as one of the annual joint initiatives for SJSU and City library staff in 2009 and a consultant was engaged to conduct an evaluation of the joint website. Usability study sessions were conducted as part of the process and it was decided that library users would be better able to find resources for their specific needs if the site was divided into a university site and a public site. Library users from both constituencies found the joint library website difficult to use. Public library users saw the website as a tool for exploration and the university faculty and students saw the website as a tool to complete specific tasks (Kizmo Inc., 2010, 37). Based on this study, separate websites have been developed for each of the library audiences, with links from each to a joint portal that explains the collaboration of the City and SJSU (www.sjlibrary.org; library.sjsu.edu; www.sjpl.org). This is an example of a feature of the joint-use library as originally planned that did not work as expected and after negotiation was redesigned.

Leadership and public tax support

Since the joint library concept was first conceived in 1996, the leadership of the City, SJSU and the respective library organizations has changed. There are a different mayor and City manager, and soon there will be a new public library director. There have been several new university presidents and provosts, and a new university library dean has been in place since 2005, arriving two years after the opening of the library. Although a number of middle managers have retired, many frontline staff and librarians involved in the planning teams for the joint-use library are still working and know and value the history of the collaboration. The challenge facing the joint-use library as it nears the first decade marker is to preserve and strengthen the partnership while allowing for innovation and transformation in response to emerging technology, new ways of learning, heightened expectations of library users and a new funding reality for both the City and the SJSU.

Public support for state-funded institutions of higher education in the state of California has dropped dramatically since the opening of the joint-use library. The CSU system is facing a possible reduction in state support, which could reduce CSU's state funding to the lowest level allocated to the university since 1996, when the CSU was serving 90,000 fewer students than in 2011-12 (CSU Budget Central, 2012). Similarly, staffing in the City public library system in the 2010-11 fiscal year fell below the 1995-96 staffing level when the system served a smaller population and had a much smaller overall circulation of materials (Light, 2011, 3). The impact of annual cuts to SJSU and City budgets and the prospect of even greater future reductions could threaten the health of the joint-use library. To date, the collaboration has weathered budget cuts to one organization or the other with flexible staffing on the part of both library staffs and the allocation of resources based upon the requirements of the operating agreement. New leadership combined with the need for re-engineering of operations and workflow to meet budget realities may even strengthen the joint-use library as we enter the second decade of its life. The shift from a print environment to a much more digital environment at this particular juncture may lead to unforeseen opportunities.

Evaluation of library services

An evaluation of the joint-use library was conducted early on in the collaboration, evaluating how the merged library served the respective communities after the merger compared to the service level prior to the merger. Two hypotheses guided the research study: that patrons perceived better quality in marker services after the merger, and that quantities of marker services delivery increased after the merger (Childers, 2006, 1-2). The overall objective of the study was to explore the impact of the merged library, compared with the individual San José Public Library and SJSU libraries prior to the merger. Surveys were conducted in the individual libraries before the merged library and then twice again during the first and second year of the joint-use library respectively. The study results showed that hypothesis 1 (quality) was not supported, with a decline in satisfaction regarding the quality of service received by some library users. Hypothesis 2 (quantity) was supported by the results of the study with the library experiencing massive gains in items circulated and patrons visiting. This study, now six years old, should be replicated to determine how both sets of constituents view the quality of service after multiple years of integrated staffing and evolving user expectations.

The university library organization has undergone two evaluation processes which looked at service to the academic community specifically. The first of these was as part of the university library five-year programme review in 2008. The purpose of the assessment, as articulated by the SJSU Academic Senate, was to ensure that the university community continued to receive high-quality services and access to collections after the establishment of the joint-use library. External reviewers of the SJSU library found that overall the King Library had proven to be successful beyond all expectations. Areas identified for improvement for the university library included enhanced communication, redesign of the website and a review of the information technology co-management structure (Butler and Dabirian, 2009, 9–10). The LibQual Service Quality Assessment (www.libqual.org) was conducted by the university library in 2009. This survey of library users' perceptions of library service qualities found SJSU library users most satisfied with community space for learning and group study, and satisfaction with the overall comfortable and inviting location. Assessed at a lower level of satisfaction was the availability of specific information resources needed to conduct academic work (http://library.sjsu.edu/library-assessment-libqual). Follow-up to both of these studies is necessary to ascertain if changes in perceptions have taken place.

The need for transformation of academic libraries

During the almost 15 years since the planning for the joint-use King Library commenced there have been major changes in the expectations of library users of both public and academic libraries. A major contributor to these changing expectations has been the role of technology in the lives of people worldwide. Use of the internet is ubiquitous across virtually all societies and the proliferation of mobile technology, particularly use of smartphones such as the iPhone, has changed the way people communicate, conduct business, learn and seek information. The manner in which people use libraries, both university and public, could not have been fully imagined by the architects and designers of the King library and so, over time, adjustments to the facility have been necessary, such as enlarging the staff workspace for the information technology department, relocating student laptop and iPad check-out services to a more visible space, adding electrical outlets for charging of mobile devices, repurposing book-stack space for library user seating, and designing library applications for mobile devices.

During the planning of the joint-use library, the biggest objection from university professors was that the general public would have print books checked out and thus make them unavailable to students and faculty who needed them for academic work. Shortly after the opening of the library, circulation of university print collections by university borrowers spiked. Not only were SJSU books not over-circulated to the general public, they were used more by SJSU students than ever before. Almost ten years later, however, the circulation of university collections by university borrowers has decreased and the circulation statistics for the general public have also declined, as the online use of e-books has significantly increased (see Table 10.3). During the 2009-10 academic year, the university's print collection of approximately 1.5 million items had a circulation among university students of approximately 175,000, while the e-book collection numbering approximately 85,000 had 750,000 online uses. The university library-users' preference for e-books over print books is clear. During the 2003-4 academic year the university library spent approximately 63% of the collections budget on print materials and 37% on digital materials. In 2010-11 the university library spent approximately 15% of the collections budget on print materials and 85% of the collections budget on digital materials.

Table 10.3 *Declining circulation of materials at the King Library*		
Patron and material type	**2004–5**	**2010–11**

Public materials
  Public patron
  SJSU patron
	1,696,368
	348,054
		943,286
		157,726

SJSU materials
  Public patron
  SJSU patron
	252,641
	237,510
		204,332
		159,274

Totals
  Public patron
  SJSU patron
	1,949,009
	585,764
		1,147,618
		316,980

Adapted with permission from San José State University Library online statistics, 2003–12, unpublished.

It has been decades since the university library has had a methodical weeding of the university print collection, owing in large part to opposition from the teaching faculty to de-accessioning of books that many believe should be archived indefinitely. With the demonstrated sharp decrease of the use of the print collection and the decreased addition of print books to the collection itself, it is time to plan for a comprehensive weeding project to identify items for withdrawal due to out-dated information, replacement with e-book format, elimination of duplicate copies, transfer to regional shared storage facilities, and other designations as may be determined. The cost to the library to house little- or never-used volumes is not sustainable and the need for seating, study and group learning spaces is ever growing. This reality coupled with the growing collections of digital book libraries such as Google Books and HathiTrust argues for a reconceptualization of the academic library as a place in a technology-rich environment.

Increasingly, it is recognized that there is a need to free up space that is now occupied by print books for new uses, for students to work, study and socialize. Other academic units such as the centre for faculty development, writing centre and other student-success support services can be co-located in the library to build on the available synergies. This is articulated in a recent publication, *Redefining the Academic Library: managing the migration to digital information services* (University Leadership Council, 2011, 48). This document has been the impetus for a CSU Library Advisory Task Force made up of provosts, faculty and library deans system-wide to explore the possibility of regional storage repositories in order to free library space for other student learning purposes.

Why are these changes in library use significant for the collaboration between the City and SJSU? First, the space allocations in the 475,000-square-foot library were originally made based on the number of volumes in and locations of the print collections. The physical space surrounding book stacks were designated as either university-owned or public-owned based on who owned the books in those stacks. So, the fifth through eighth floors were designated as 100% university library space and the third floor was designated as 100% public library space because of the ownership of the book collections on those floors. Second, shared spaces were designated in those areas where the libraries shared service desks and collections, such as the reference collection and the periodicals collection. What happens to the space allocation formula when the university library begins to take down the stacks with a need to repurpose the space for student learning activities? Or when the public library has need to reconfigure spaces because of changing needs? What happens if and when the service desks such as the reference desk cease to serve as the primary locus for service?

Another issue that would be impacted by a significant decrease in the size of the university print collection is the possibility of collaborating on the implementation of a Radio Frequency Identification (RFID) technology system. The public library organization has proposed and initiated planning for the implementation of an RFID system for the public library system including the main library and all of the 22 branch libraries. Collaborating on the costs and implementation for RFID between the public and university library would be advantageous since the joint-use library currently has a shared integrated library system, circulation system, self-check units, security tagging and theft-detection gates. The public library collection housed in the 22 branches numbers 2,270,645 items (San José Public

Library, 2010-11). Although e-books are being added to both the public library collection and the university collection, the public library continues to provide a large volume of new print books throughout the main library and all of the branch libraries making technologically enhanced collection management and maintenance essential for efficient staffing allocation throughout the system.

As previously discussed, the print book collection is declining in use and cost effectiveness to the university community, with university students and faculty preferring to find information in digital format, including online articles, e-books and e-journals, and streaming audio and video. For the university library to participate in the most responsible way in the RFID project, the collections would need to be weeded prior to the actual tagging of the books, so as to not waste funds on books that could soon be discarded or moved to regional shared storage. The process for planning and implementing a programmatic weeding project will happen over time, and so waiting for that to happen would hamper the efforts of the public library to better manage their collections and decrease the number of staff in that process. Negotiations on the issue of RFID implementation are imminent.

Conclusion

As the ethos of both the university and the public library become more digital and ubiquitous within the library users' lives, how will joint-use King Library spaces be utilized? Both communities need gathering places, communal learning sites and civic affairs spaces where individuals can interact with information and information consultants either face to face or virtually. Will the physical space as it is now designated continue to be within the jurisdiction of one library or the other? Will the digital presence of the two libraries become a virtual joint space? Will the digital library for the university become embedded within the university's course management system and thus become less of a distinct identified library space? How will the university embed itself within the community? These are far-reaching questions that it is time to tackle so that the library collaboration between SJSU and the City can continue as the 21st century continues to be shaped by exponential advances in technology. The time to plan for 2027, 15 years hence, is now.

References

Bundy, A. (2003) Joint-Use Libraries: the ultimate form of cooperation. In McCabe, G. and Kennedy, J. (eds), *Planning the Modern Public Library Building*, Libraries Unlimited.

Butler, B. and Dabirian, A. (2009) San José State University, Dr. Martin Luther King Jr. Library, University Library Programme Review, unpublished.

California State University (CSU) Budget Central (2012) *CSU Budget Central,* http://blogs.calstate.edu/budgetcentral.

Childers, T. (2006) *San José's King Library Metrics Project: impacts of the merger. Final report,* unpublished.

City of San José (2012) *City Facts Brochure,* www.sanjoseca.gov/about.asp.

Fleming, C. (2012) A Joint University Library: vision and reality, *Library Management,* **33** (1), 95-103.

Gomez, E., Hulthen, E. and Drehmer, U. (1998) Harnosand, Sweden, *Public Library Quarterly,* **31** (4), 22-4.

Keene, J. and Fairman, R. (2011) Building an Integrated Workforce through Shared Values: the Worcester Library and History Center, *Library Review,* **60** (3), 188-201.

Kifer, R. (2007) The Dr Martin Luther King Jr. Library: public policy in action in Silicon Valley USA. In Bundy, A. (ed.), *Joint Use Libraries: an international conference held on 19-21 June 2007,* Auslib Press Pty Ltd.

Kizmo, Inc. (2010) San José Library Web Site Usability Study, unpublished.

Light, J. (2011) *2010-2011 Annual Library Usage Report,* report to the City of San José Library Commission, unpublished.

MacDougall, H. and Quinlan, N. (2001) Staffing Challenges for a Joint-Use Library: the Nova Southeastern University and Broward County experience. In Miller, W. and Pellen, R. (eds), *Joint-Use Libraries,* Haworth Information Press.

McNicol, S. (2008) *Joint-Use Libraries: libraries for the future,* Chandos Publishing.

Moll, M. (2010) First Mergers: a case study of the Boland College of Education and the Capre Technikon Libraries, *South African Journal of Library & Information Science,* **76** (1), 57-63.

Mudd, S. and Havens, A. (2009) Combining Forces to Achieve More: library cooperation in the 21st century, *Next Space, the OCLC Newsletter,* **12,** 4-9.

Office of the County Auditor (2007) *Nova Southeastern University Joint-Use Library Agreement: review of reported public usage,* Report 07-15, Broward County Florida.

Peterson, C. (2004) The Martin Luther King, Jr. Library: a joint-use library as an urban educational corridor, *Metropolitan Universities: International Forum,* **15** (3), 30-40.

San José Mercury News (1997) The Library Card Mayor has a Brilliant Plan for San José State Partnership, *San José Mercury News,* 4 February, 6B.

San José Public Library (2010-11) *Facts at a Glance,* City of San José.

San José State University Office of Institutional Research (2012) *Institutional Effectiveness & Analytics,* www.oir.sjsu.edu.

Thompson, S. (2004) Marketing before Opening San José's Dual-Purpose Library, *Marketing Library Services,* **18** (6).

University Leadership Council (2011) *Redefining the Academic Library: managing the migration to digital information services*, Advisory Board Company.

Index